THE LONE RANGER AND BUDDHA

D1643270

"Remembering that a neutral mask class in college was one of the few acting exercises I found really useful, I was curious to see how an accomplished actor like Peter Coyote would tie mask work to the tenets of Buddhist philosophy. Through the lens of the Lone Ranger and Tonto, Coyote cleverly conveys the message of finding oneself by losing oneself. I highly recommend this book to every actor—veteran or fledgling—indeed to every human who has ever felt constrained by the voices of self-criticism in their head."

JEAN SMART, EMMY AWARD–WINNING ACTOR

"This pithy book is flat-out brilliant. It weaves together deep Buddhist teaching, the magic of improv and mask work, and a compelling dialogue between three iconic characters, each of whom represent an aspect of the spiritual path. Only Peter Coyote in all his facets and talents could have written this book. I'm glad he did."

LEWIS RICHMOND, AUTHOR OF *AGING AS A SPIRITUAL PRACTICE*

"In a world full of ideas about getting the advantage, gaining the edge or greater power, and improving your position or standing, it is so *utterly refreshing* to have a master speak of liberation from our long-standing ego conundrums to acknowledge and invite energy from the beyond to flow through, shape, and inform our thoughts, action, and speech. Story, masks, meditation—by all means—you are you before you have a thought, and you have the freedom to manifest the person, to wear the *mask,* of your choosing. Go ahead! Drop the striving and have some fun with this play of language brought forth by the wily Coyote."

EDWARD ESPE BROWN, ZEN PRIEST AND
AUTHOR OF *THE TASSAJARA BREAD BOOK*

"In *The Lone Ranger and Tonto Meet Buddha,* I spent time not just with masks but with the craft of masking as a method of becoming more awake. I entered mask classes and met not only the teacher and the teaching but the students and what they were getting out of it. In this book are solid Buddhist commentary, intriguing story, and from that mix, I sense an emerging American discipline that unites theater and dharma—the Way of the Mask."

DAVID CHADWICK, AUTHOR OF *CROOKED CUCUMBER:*
THE LIFE AND ZEN TEACHING OF SHUNRYU SUZUKI

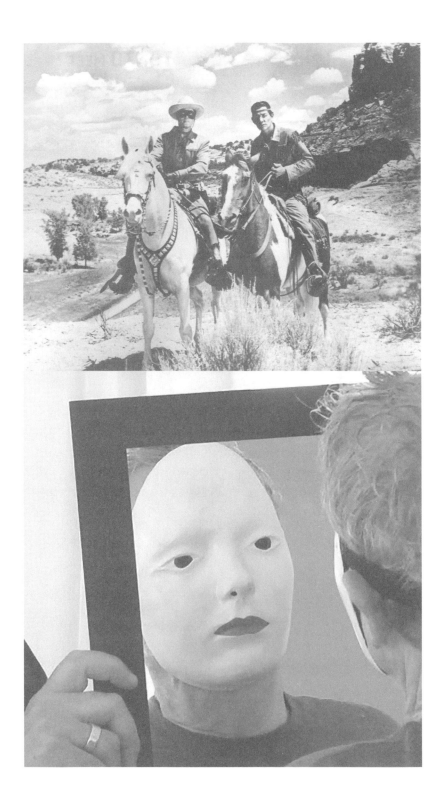

THE **LONE RANGER** AND **TONTO** MEET **BUDDHA**

Masks,
Meditation, and
Improvised Play
to Induce
Liberated States

PETER COYOTE

Inner Traditions
Rochester, Vermont

Inner Traditions
One Park Street
Rochester, Vermont 05767
www.InnerTraditions.com

Text stock is SFI certified

Cataloging-in-Publication Data for this title is available from the Library of Congress

ISBN 978-1-64411-356-1 (print)
ISBN 978-1-64411-357-8 (ebook)

Printed and bound in the United States by Lake Book Manufacturing, Inc.
The text stock is SFI certified. The Sustainable Forestry Initiative® program
promotes sustainable forest management.

10 9 8 7 6 5 4 3 2 1

Text design and layout by Debbie Glogover
This book was typeset in Garamond Premier Pro with Gill Sans MT Pro,
ITC Legacy Sans Std, and Gineso used as display typefaces

To send correspondence to the author of this book, mail a first-class letter to the
author c/o Inner Traditions • Bear & Company, One Park Street, Rochester, VT
05767, and we will forward the communication, or contact the author directly at
www.petercoyote.com.

For Dick Grace, the Marine of compassion,
always storming the next hill.
Semper Fi.
Not negotiable. Not Relative.
Absolute!
and
Keith Johnstone, the quietest,
shyest genius I have ever known.

I expect original words from you. But we have to be careful at this point. This word must be expressed by a person who comes to the same mind as Shakyamuni Buddha. . . . Then the original American way can be naturally realized.

YAMADA MUMON-ROSHI,
"LECTURE," IN *WIND BELL* (1976)

We only have two alternatives; we either take everything for sure and real, or we don't. If we follow the first, we end up bored to death with ourselves and with the world. If we follow the second and erase personal history, we create a fog around us, a very exciting and mysterious state in which nobody knows where the rabbit will pop out, not even ourselves.

DON JUAN MATUS, IN CARLOS CASTANEDA,
A SEPARATE REALITY

We can achieve enlightenment only through the practice of meditation; without it there is no way we can transform our minds.

DALAI LAMA,
AWAKENING THE MIND, LIGHTENING THE HEART

Contents

PART TWO

Keeping Your Learning Accessible

A True Holiday
from Self-Consciousness

The organizing principle of my work as a Buddhist teacher and an instructor in these mask workshops is personal transformation. While I cherish the utility and transcendental power of mask work, it's important to reiterate that, compared with consistent meditation practice and the implications of Buddha's understanding, mask experiences resemble the temporary gas flares of psychedelics more than the geologic vistas of enduring terrain. Taking psychedelics or wearing masks definitely alters perspectives, temporarily suppresses the ego, and engenders the liberation accompanying that suppression. They offer the novel shock of perceiving anew a world one had previously considered known and fixed. But such experiences also have a shadow.

Compared with the obdurate weight of our habits, one night's expanded mind experience will eventually be reburied beneath the repetitive weight of our normal attachments and habits. If you make your own way to the "Grand Canyon"—the transcendental experience— by meditating, strengthening the body, and analyzing habits of daily thoughts and impulses, you will be able to return on your own steam by following clues and route markers assembled during the journey. Failing that, you remain dependent on the transport that carried you, such as the drug or the mask—a reliance outside one's control.

While I've attempted to minimize Buddhist philosophy in these pages, it's nearly impossible to remake the way we perceive the world and fix these positive changes without understanding insights the Buddha stressed in his teachings. For those interested in deep transformation and repeat excursions to freedom, such changes require challenging habitual (usually unconscious) premises and assumptions. Both meditation practice and Buddhist thought are tools precisely calibrated to aid serious students in mastering those challenges.

WHY THIS BOOK?

For readers confronted with thousands of spiritual texts, ranging from the "I channel a dead guy and he tells us what to do" variety to accurate explanations of spiritual traditions and practices, they might wonder why they should read *this* book. My self-serving but accurate reply would be that the exercises and games inside it are designed and proven to offer the peak experience of self-less freedom, a true holiday from self-consciousness, which always brings with it an experience of freedom and joy, whether or not that person has ever considered him- or herself spiritual.

My interest lies in approaching liberation through experiences that don't appear foreign to everyday Americans of any background, are not larded with too many foreign words and exotic costumes, and are practices that can be carried on in your daily life without arousing undue attention. My predilection is to have fun, and most people find fun irresistible.

The parable of the Lone Ranger, Tonto, and the Buddha interspersed in these pages translates many of the experiences in the text into recognizable human afflictions with good humor but with a serious intent to help readers see themselves in these characters.

Whether or not Buddhism eventually interests you, it is not a requisite for enjoying and using this book. However, for those who might become inspired to seek more permanent transformation and understand Buddhism in greater depth, the bibliography offers reliable sources of information.

Even if you choose never to practice meditation or explore Buddhist thought, you will be changed, positively, by this work. You will be more intuitive, less fearful of the judgments of others, more spontaneous, and more able to fearlessly commit to your own choices in life. In the same way, as we (author and reader) travel together, the masked man will come to realize the limitations that his mask (and his mask of a self) have imposed on him. It's my hope that you will make the effort to understand and enjoy the freedom that derives from knowing that all your own masks are simply faces of the formless energy of the universe, rising and falling like ocean waves, apparently discrete but never, ever free of the ocean.

Any personal problem bears a direct relationship to ideas we hold about ourselves. I say *ideas* because over time humans tend to solidify ideas and information they've received about themselves into a fixed identity. When that occurs, life becomes restricted, options disappear, and a great deal of joy evaporates.

The games and exercises in the first half of this book have been culled from forty-five years of Zen practice and my ordination as a priest and an equal amount of time and study as an actor. These games and exercises will reward you with liberation from unreasonable self-doubts, doublethinking, shyness, and fear. They will teach you how to let your ego (your sense of self) take a break and relinquish its constant state of being on guard, strategizing, and problem solving. From that point, it becomes easier to calm the mind's hyperactivity and discipline our self-importance and allow spontaneous playfulness and spaciousness to express itself as the play of our deepest nature. Once such states are experienced in a cold, sober environment, it engenders tremendous confidence in the existence of freedom, previously only imagined.

I draft that confidence, for the second half of the book, to will students to integrate this feeling of freedom and confidence into their daily life. The second part is dedicated to clarifying and explaining Zen Buddhist theory and practice in clear, simple language for Americans who may not consider themselves religious or spiritual. No worries!

It takes about half a day of preparation, but then, by placing a neutral mask over your face and regarding this new face in a mirror, your sense of self will be temporarily displaced. The spirit of the mask (which is actually your own mind) can ride you like a kayaker negotiating a torrent, *using* but not controlling the power propelling it. Each encounter with a mask generates a new, fully dimensional holographic personality you will instantaneously "know" intimately, in the same way that you understand and intuit events in dreams. Under its influence, you will not be burdened by your habitual limitations. Repeating the experience with different masks will afford incontrovertible evidence of the boundary-less freedom lurking just beyond the edges of who you've defined yourself to be. A visceral experience of an alternate self will make you wonder what suddenly happened to the old you.

Like a psychedelic drug trip on LSD, ayahuasca, mushrooms, peyote, or San Pedro cactus, the experience will end when you remove the mask. However, a residue will remain, a palpable feeling that the world is more magical and boundless than you had conceived. The Zen practices explained in the book's second half will teach you how to recover those positive experiences and bind them to your life as permanent habits.

Mask work will not enlighten you and fix every problem in your life (neither will *enlightenment*), but you can think of mask work (Buddhist descriptions of reality) as encouragement that these states of mind actually exist and you experienced them without the use of drugs. These experiences—via mask or drug—function in the same way mystical experiences can arise during meditation. The mystical moments are not the goal but serve as signposts, acknowledging the right direction and providing encouragement to remain on the path.

🔯 🔯 🔯

The unavoidable challenge of discussing enlightened states and techniques for experiencing them in print involves clarifying *perceptions* that
exist beyond the limits of language. An early Zen monk's response to
his teacher's challenge to express his insight poses the problem clearly:
"If I open my mouth, I lie. If I don't speak, I'm a coward."

Just as one could write instructions for riding a bicycle, experiences
described on paper may appear to be clear and comprehensible but can
be perceived and mastered only through practice. Buddhist teaching and
practice have certified the reality of enlightenment (though I prefer the
Zen term *kensho,* which means "seeing into one's own nature") for 2,500
years, during which time that knowledge has been passed down from
certified teachers to students until today. As a part of my transmission
ceremony, I was tasked with copying the name of every known disciple of
the Buddha (in my lineage), all the way back to the time of the Buddha,
2,500 years ago. My Buddhist name (Hosho Jishi, which means "dharma
voice, compassion warrior") is the last name on that list.

As Americans, we have received Buddha's teachings in the gift
wrapping of various cultures that previously hosted this knowledge—
India, China, Tibet, Japan, Vietnam, Indonesia, and so forth. Each of
those cultures expressed the Buddha's gift in aesthetics and ceremonies
appropriate to its own traditions and customs. Because these expressions
appear exotic and intriguing to us, there is a danger that we begin to
associate spirituality with arcane, ceremonial, and often obscure practices that are cultural but not universal.

In its homeland of Nepal, Buddhism evolved from Hindu culture, and part of its gift wrapping included Hinduism's belief in rein-
carnation and multiple rebirths. In ancient China, Buddhism melded
with Taoism and Confucianism to produce many schools of Buddhist
thought, including Chan, which is the Chinese precursor to Japanese
Zen. In Tibet, the practices were annealed with the native Bon shamanism to produce the various Tibetan Buddhist cults and wiggy ceremonies. In Japan, Buddhism married native Shinto and cultural practices
to produce Zen.

These exotic expressions are the masks Buddhism has chosen to harmonize with these cultures. Some ceremonies and practices may or may not be central to the core wisdom—the real gift—that has been transmitted across the generations. In America today, there are many expressions of Buddhism adopted from many cultures, but we can't really conclude that Buddhism has taken root in America until an American expression of it, one that does not feel foreign to most citizens, has been born. (This is not to disparage any stage of its evolution to date but to remind us that we are observing a young sapling, not a fully formed and mature tree.) This is the deeper implication of Yamada Mumon-roshi's quote at the beginning of the book.

One purpose of this book is to loosen the gift wrappings in which Buddhism has been delivered to us so that Americans can more readily identify the actual gifts—dependent origination, the Four Noble Truths, and the Eightfold Path—and the practice of meditation, which orients us to them.

Dependent origination is the Buddhist doctrine of interdependence of all phenomena in the world. I am particularly indebted to David Brazier for his translation and analysis of the Four Noble Truths that follow. The Four Noble Truths are the truths that are the first of all Truths, meaning "real." They are noble because they must be respected, dignified, and faced courageously. The first is that suffering exists (*dukkha,* understood as "affliction"). According to Buddha birth is dukkha, so is death, sickness, wanting things to be different, wanting unpleasant events to end. Dukkha is the reality of life and unavoidable.

We do not suffer because we are somehow ignorant or at fault. It is not shameful. The Second Noble Truth, *sudhayana,* means "arising," indicating that contact with dukkha will produce emotions and strong feelings in the mind. (However, it is also energy.) This explains that suffering has a cause. The Third Noble Truth, *nirodha,* comes from the Sanskrit word meaning to bank a fire, to contain it. Uncontrolled fire, like uncontrolled passions, are a danger, so containing our powerful thoughts and emotions through meditation and discipline is why Buddha can proclaim that suffering has an end. It is NOT that Enlightenment somehow ends dukkha. The Buddha sickened and died after his Enlightenment. He means that it teaches us how to live in a world that will afflict us between birth and death. The "how" to live is the Eightfold Path, a series of moral practices and mindfulness techniques that transforms our powerful feelings into the core of an enlightened life. The first of the eight is *right understanding;* however, the word *right* is not to meant to be understood as the opposite of wrong. To avoid right being construed to mean the correct or only way—and following my teacher's practice—I substitute the word *Buddhist* for *right,* which signifies that this is *our* way and not necessarily the only way. The Eightfold Path consists of Buddhist understanding, Buddhist thought, Buddhist speech (no gossip, lies, slander), Buddhist action, Buddhist livelihood, Buddhist effort, Buddhist mindfulness, and Buddhist concentration.[1]

It's my hope that such unpacking might encourage a more intimate union with our American culture until the aura of something "foreign" and "exotic" is absorbed and transformed by an American expression. Buddha's discoveries are universally true for all people and are available to any human on Earth. His genius, over and above achieving complete perfect enlightenment, was to make it comprehensible to the Hindu culture in which he was raised, while disregarding that culture's prejudices against women and untouchables and its division between secular and religious ideas and castes or classes of people.

My hope is to share this understanding with American people who may never wear robes, chant Japanese translations of Pali, shave their heads, or do full prostrations. My belief in humans' natural compassion, curiosity, and search for knowledge leads me to believe that Americans will discover and exploit the great and useful tool Buddha has delivered to humankind. But let's begin with the fun!

PART ONE

FINDING THE SECRETS

I hate improv . . . when forced to do it, I get anxious and in my head. I had never worked with masks, but when I put one on and looked at my image in a mirror, a body movement came to me . . . I employed that movement, and my body registered the effect; it was as if I had suddenly stabilized on a surfboard. . . . I hid behind the mask, became the character I had just instantly created with the body movement, and [everything] just sort of flowed. It's the first time I've ever gotten anything out of improv, and I can totally use this technique. Actually, I already purchased my own mask for that very purpose!

KEITH CONTI, WORKSHOP PARTICIPANT

1
Losing Myself

In 1955 I was fourteen, and I became fascinated by the rebellious adults of the Beat Generation and their criticisms of American culture. Hearing adults express and clarify feelings I was experiencing as a teenager—the political repression of the McCarthy period (which affected my family personally) and the culture's fascination with materialism, its racism, and its obviously biased economic and judicial systems—spurred me to read and study Beat authors and poets such as Jack Kerouac, Allen Ginsberg, Gary Snyder, Lew Welch, Philip Whalen, and others. Their interest in Zen led me to a book, *The Three Pillars of Zen* by Philip Kapleau, which offered me a thrilling (though perhaps romanticized) introduction to Zen and enlightenment. This book planted a hardy evergreen in the soil of my imagination.

Zen is the Japanese translation of the Chinese word *chan,* which means "meditation." Zen differs from other schools of Buddhism by being, in the words of Zen master Norman Fischer, who many years later became a role model and friend:

A pithy, stripped-down, determined, uncompromising, cut-to-the-chase, meditation-based Buddhism that takes no interest in doctrinal refinements. Not relying on scripture, doctrine or ritual, Zen is verified by personal experience and is passed on from master to disciple, hand to hand, ineffably, through hard, intimate training.[1]

This seemed perfect for me, but what did I know? The Beats dug it, and they were cool and adult. That was sufficient pedigree.

Introduced to the concept of enlightenment, I began to see it as the light at the end of the tunnel of my adolescence—a heady possibility to a sexually obsessed teenage boy, clad in baby fat, lousy at sports, afraid of his father, and tongue-tied around girls. Enlightenment would be the key to unlock every mystery, make me immune to the ridicule of classmates, and free me to understand the undecipherable utterances of the Zen masters I encountered in my reading. An instance:

> Tanzan and Ekido were once traveling together down a muddy road. A heavy rain was still falling. Coming around a bend, they met a lovely girl in a silk kimono and sash, unable to cross the flooded intersection.
>
> "Come on, girl," said Tanzan at once. Lifting her in his arms, he carried her over the mud. Ekido did not speak again until that night when they reached a lodging temple. Then he could no longer restrain himself.
>
> "We monks don't go near females," he told Tanzan, "especially not young and lovely ones like that girl back there. It is dangerous. Why did you do that?"
>
> "I left the girl back there," said Tanzan. "Why are you still carrying her?"

I began to read everything I could on the subject and was soon anesthetizing my playmates with facile explanations of Buddhist philosophy, quoting Zen maxims as if I understood them, and imagining myself a hair's breath away from "highest, perfect, enlightenment," without ever having met a Buddhist. I was matriculating in my own unaccredited university as a poseur.

After college, I moved to San Francisco to pursue a master's degree in creative writing, studying with a poet I admired named Robert Duncan. However, graduate school paled next to the allure of the emerging counterculture, and after my first term and a tepid season with a local theater whose cream of management and talent had been siphoned off to New York to found Lincoln Center, I auditioned and was accepted in a radical street theater company named the San Francisco Mime Troupe.

Mime is not to be confused with pantomime, which, as exemplified by Marcel Marceau and numerous whiteface street performers, creates the illusion of objects in space. Mime as taught by Etienne Decroux, the teacher of the troupe's founder, R. G. Davis, uses objects to express ideas: an umbrella might become a rifle, a pool cue, or a broom, and a mime troupe very definitely uses *speech* to convey issues and ideas.

The troupe's vision was to employ theater, particularly comedy, to further progressive political goals. We performed in the city's parks, bringing our theater to the people in the tradition of seventeenth-century Italian *commedia dell'arte* (think human Punch and Judy). Our improvised, bawdy tomfoolery skewered officials, the pompous, and the rich and famous (as the original *commedias* did). We were enthusiastically appreciated and supported by our audiences, who dropped money in the hats we passed around after performances.

The troupe used traditional Italian masked characters—Pantalone (the miser), Dottore (the know-it-all blowhard), Harlequino (the amorous clown), and the unmasked, clever, not-so-innocent maidservant—comic archetypes that have survived the centuries. We repurposed them to address contemporary events.

Our plays featured flirtatious women, risqué décolletage, pratfalls, double entendres, and lovers fleeing through bedroom windows as husbands entered through doors. The action and dialogue were punctuated by abundant physical play known as *lazzi* (lahd-zee)—short, very precise bits of comic business that required precise skill and perfect timing. Over and above our success, adventures, and rising celebrity status, as the troupe's reputation grew, the most startling and enduring experience, one that changed me profoundly, was my introduction to masks.

Ten years before I began my formal study of Buddhism, the day I first performed in a mask, ignited a flame that never lost its heat and glow. Fifty-two years later, I can vividly recall the moment I *became* Pantalone, my favorite character to this day. I was costumed in his long robes and a codpiece over a red union suit. When I put on the mask, the little goatee of braided rope, and his cap and assumed his traditional hunched-over posture before a mirror, he clicked into holographic focus in my imagination. What a surprise! He spoke the Yiddish-inflected English of my grandfather.

He was cranky, rude, blustering, blasphemous, sly, treacherous, and wicked, and I loved him at first encounter. All the attributes I had scrubbed from my personality, trying to become a mature and good person, were obliterated by Pantalone's raw vitality, blunt desires, and boundary-less amorality.

The first time Pantalone introduced his whiny, indulged daughter to the audience, an improvised line whizzed from Pantalone's psyche straight out through my mouth: "De reason I luv my dawta [*a pause and, then, with glee*] is dat she killed my vife in childboith."

Tasteless and inappropriate, I know, but when hurled from the safe venue of a stage, the audience howled with delight—and I had somehow "known" they would before I'd uttered a word.

Behind that mask, I could do no wrong. My familiar self was no longer hovering over my shoulder, criticizing and editing my behavior, insisting on accepting social norms, insisting that I be good, kind, and considerate. Whenever I donned Pantalone's mask, Peter Cohon (my born name) vanished from my inner landscape. My good manners, sensitivity, and anxieties about what people would think dissipated like steam. What remained was Pantalone—a living, feral id, operating without regard to correctness, social convention, limits, self-judgment, or fear. I had never before experienced such unconstrained freedom, and it became an immediate addiction.

Author as Pantalone
(photo credit: Erik Weber)

PANTALONE

Whenever I encountered an onstage (and sometimes offstage) situation that made Peter "the actor" uncomfortable, it was clear to me that my housebroken self had regained control. I learned to dive into those discomfort zones, refusing to shy away from them, and, little by little, developed the courage to allow Pantalone access to the widest spectrum of impulses and images passing through my spinal telephone. It was a practice I'd developed during numerous psychedelic experiences where, on the verge of some emotional or mental difficulty, I strived to consciously face the fear or discomfort and enjoy it. In every case, the event mutated into something pleasurable.

There is energy in fear and discomfort if you can remain steadfast when it seizes you. Colonized by Pantalone's spirit, I was no longer the known quantity of Robert Peter Cohon, a middle-class Jewish boy from Englewood, New Jersey. His values (and my parents' values and judgments) no longer applied in the magical, boundary-less kingdom ruled by Pantalone.

Freedom from fear allowed me to make startling choices onstage and surprising pivots, unencumbered by doubt. Relieved of my own personality, I could do *anything* in my mask, and it was enthralling fun! Acting behind the mask was not a delusional trance. It was still necessary to remain fully alert to the script, the other actors, and offstage accidents, which it was my duty to acknowledge and fold into the play. All that was missing was my old familiar self. It is the purpose of this book and the classes from which this method arose to offer others this same freedom and explain and solidify with explanations and practices I have learned in my forty-five-year study of Zen.

A NOT-TOO-SERIOUS PARABLE ABOUT A MASKED MAN

The Lone Ranger had lost all track of time. He hadn't washed in days, and his lips were cracked from the desert sun. Every once in a while, he'd catch the scent of himself, which was strong enough to kill fleas. It could have been weeks, months, or years that he and Tonto had been circling this trackless wasteland, enduring the blistering heat, thirst, and fatigue for reasons he could no longer remember. At first, they'd been chasing Blackheart Bud, but the Lone Ranger remembered killing him and returning the widow's money. Then there was that mean, quick-gun kid from Dodge City, throwing his weight around, shooting dogs, and scaring the citizens. He was fast but not accurate, and the Lone Ranger's silver .44 slug literally blew him out of his boots. There'd been a fuss. He could remember that—the boy's weeping mother declaring that "he was only a kid." The Lone Ranger had countered with Wild Bill Hickok's famous comeback to the mother of a fourteen-year-old he'd just eliminated: "Madam, a boy can pull a trigger as well as a man."

After that, he couldn't seem to find the thread of how they'd arrived where they were and in such sorry condition, looking like a couple of rag merchants. The series had ended; no new scripts (or paychecks) had come in. He still had no idea how they'd return to Los Angeles. It *must have been after 1952 because that was the year of the big career squabble when he complained about their measly $500-a-week salary despite his being a huge star.*

"The company raked in all the loot," he remembered bitterly. "I demanded a fair share, and they hired some doofus to be me. The Wrather Corporation took me to court and forbid me from bein' the Lone Ranger, even off-screen, and I had to wait till the company's rat-bag president died before I could even wear my mask again."

He cut off that train of thought. Tonto was right. Thinking like that didn't serve him, but changing his mind didn't help either, and things were pretty desperate. He knew he was the Lone Ranger, no matter what any judge declared. "I knew how to be the Lone Ranger, and they didn't," he reminded himself fervently. He knew the world needed good men to fight evil, so he didn't see any reason to stop, movies or no movies. Reflexively, he checked his watch, but he had forgotten to wind it long ago.

He looked over at Tonto, worried. Somewhere along the way, his buckskins had gotten tattered and stained, and he'd thrown on one of those black hoodies, like a ghetto kid. He was slouched over the saddle like it was too much trouble to sit up straight. His standards were slipping. "That's how we lose it," the Lone Ranger mused, "letting the little things slide." He rubbed his jaw and realized he hadn't shaved in days. "Gotta make a note to do that," he thought, but he had no pencil and couldn't remember where he'd last seen his razor.

Silver had gone lame in his right front foot, and the off rhythm made the Lone Ranger jumpy. He looked down at the saggy cloth billowing out of his stained white shirt and the stretched unkempt fit of his custom moleskin trousers. "I must have lost 25 pounds," he mused, and he was glad there were no kids around to see him in this state. He slipped back into bitterness again. "Nobody gives a shit about the Lone Ranger anymore. It's these DC Comic weirdos and their superpowers. Nothing human there. Why bother?"

Tonto kept his own counsel. Everywhere he looked there was only dry hardpan, sage brush, and mesas. He missed the deep greens of Mohawk country in Upstate New York and Canada, the oaks, hickories, hemlocks, and firs. He missed the company and the sweat lodges of his people, the teasing and banter, and the lustrous, high-cheek-boned girls who eluded his grasp. "It's all rust and anemia here," he observed.

There was barely enough feed for their horses, and both Scout and Silver were ratty and unkempt. "It ain't the glory days," he mused. "What happened to my thoroughbreds? Drinking Chivas at the track? I had a gorgeous wife and three kids. Those producers thought I didn't know that Tonto *meant 'stupid' in Spanish. Them that did, when they tried to get under my skin, I just smiled, banked my checks, and never gave 'em a second thought . . . most of the time."*

"I was a star," *he remembered. "How many skins can say that? I wasn't a* white *star, but plenty of women threw themselves at me. All the Mohawk people knew me. Hell, every skin knew me everywhere I went. Now they're watching stupid shit about four white kids in an apartment. That's somebody's idea of life, I guess."*

The memory generated a sour, coppery taste in his mouth, which he tried to smother with a cigarette, sucking the acrid smoke deep into his lungs as if it might purify him from the inside. It was on that thought that he saw a little curl of smoke rising from a copse of cottonwoods about a quarter mile away. A single man was sitting before a tiny fire. "Kemosabe," he said, and when he got the Lone Ranger's attention, he gestured with his chin in the camp's direction.

"Let's go check it out," the Lone Ranger said, and neck-reined Silver in that direction.

I eventually left the mime troupe with a number of my colleagues to dedicate ourselves more fully to revolutionary cultural change. We formed a group called the Diggers, imagining a world we would like to live in and *actualizing* it by acting it out. We fed four hundred to six hundred people a day for free in Golden Gate Park during the blossoming of the Haight-Ashbury district in San Francisco, established the first free medical clinic with weekly visits by doctors in our Free Store, which offered clothing, furniture, tools, televisions, bicycles, and whatever to the public for free. The unstated question behind the Free Store was: "Why become an employee so that you can become a consumer? We'll give you the stuff for free. Now, what do you want to do?" We used theatrical devices and improvisatory skills to create institutions we felt would allow people alternatives to having to be employees and consumers.[2]

During that decade, I had the good fortune to meet and become friends with Gary Snyder, one of the Beat poets I'd been reading in my teens. Gary was already famous by then, a "first among equals" among the Beats, distinguished not only by his talent as a world-class poet-scholar but also as an environmental thinker and essayist. Gary had just returned to California after spending nine years practicing in a Zen monastery in Japan as an assistant to the head teacher. He spoke and wrote Japanese fluently and had married a Japanese woman. If anyone knew what Zen was about, I thought, it would be him.

Our first meeting, arranged by a mutual friend, was disappointing to me because Gary somehow overlooked the fact that I was an enlightened Zen peer. He appeared relatively uninterested in any of my radical politics and scrutinized me calmly, with a directness and depth I found disconcerting. The memory of my uneasiness needled me to meet him again and perhaps observe more carefully how a "Zen guy" lived.

Eventually, a friendship developed between us that included wide-ranging conversations where a single question of mine might provoke an erudite response crossing continents and centuries. Afternoons were consumed in this way. I was way out of my depth in his company, but over the thud of axes and the gravelly plaints of our chain saws, I persisted, while we trimmed trees and brush on Gary's land in the foothills of the Sierra Mountains.

Over time I came to understand that Gary's breadth of knowledge was not only vast and scholarly but also impeccably organized. He could speak at length on subjects as diverse as free rock climbing, Native American cultures and beliefs of widely different Native nations, Buddhism as expressed across multiple cultures, Asian art, geology, logging, carpentry, mountain climbing, and in-depth cultural and political appraisals of many lands. He had, upon his return from Japan, enlisted a crew, with friends of mine among them, who, under his instruction, built a wonderful log home—an architectural cross between a Japanese farmhouse and a Native American longhouse constructed of timber grown on his land.[3]

It required some years before I was able to pinpoint the most compelling and elusive quality of Gary's personality: he was the first person I had ever met who appeared to be *evenly developed* across every dimension of his life. I resolved to learn something about that.

About ten years after I met Gary, I courted and later married a woman who was practicing at the San Francisco Zen Center. Though I had been reading about Zen since my early teens, I had no idea what degree of attention and diligence was required to meditate in a traditional Zen practice situation. Under my girlfriend's influence, I began "sitting" regularly and realized immediately (and painfully) that my ideas about Buddhism had missed not just the mark but the entire target.

It required less than a month of tearing myself out of bed at 5:30 a.m. to be on my cushion in the zendo, the room where zazen, or sitting meditation, is practiced, before the bells chimed. It was humiliating to discover that I was unable to meditate without fidgeting and could not seem to locate the correct place in the morning chant book before the chant had ended and a new one had begun, which I also could not locate. I could not seem to remember to bow to others (whether or not I liked them), nor could I refrain from inserting myself in conversations before my opinion had been solicited. I continually stumbled over subtle details of mindful practice, like entering a room by stepping through doorways with the foot closest to the hinge first. The daily humiliation of repetitive, public errors bludgeoned me with embarrassment until I was forced to admit how callow my ideas about Zen were.

I was saved from fleeing the monastery by a mélange of pride, fear of failure, competitiveness, and deep curiosity. That combo impelled me to keep struggling until somehow I discovered myself in the stream, which is accepting my life as it actually is, a practice I have followed to this day. I am not the man I imagined I might be but perhaps am closer to the man I actually wanted to be even though my current identity resists definition. The truth is I no longer have much of an idea of *who* I am and remain consistently grateful for that. "Not knowing" and the consequent surprise of discovering every day, moment by moment, who it is that arises now is like a return to a long-forgotten innocence.

2

The Wheel's Spinning,
but the Gerbil's Gone

Knowledge arrives in many different vessels and under many different flags. When I began my practice at the San Francisco Zen Center, like most converts I assumed it was the ultimate expression of Buddhism. I learned to love the rigor, the forms, and the aesthetics, and despite their sometimes being a bit tangential to my everyday American life, I felt as if I'd come home. I loved my Japanese meditating clothes—loose and comfortable and fashionably black—and I began to nurse a slightly pitiful belief in Zen's superiority to all other practices. As my daughter put it to me once, "Dad, you've swallowed the Kool-Aid" (a reference, for those too young to know, to the mass suicide of nine hundred people in a cult commune run by Jim Jones, an early San Francisco New Age "guru").

Life happens. Work took me far afield from the San Francisco Zen Center, and I had to adjust to its demands and different cultures and settings. The one constant that remained was my meditation, and gradually my attachment to it superseded most other loyalties as my confidence in meditation grew.

I learned that in a curious way. Nearly twenty years ago, I was rebuilding an old truck, a 1952 Dodge Power Wagon. The people helping me ran a shop in Fairfield, Iowa, called Vintage Power Wagons, and they were experts in the field and had three acres of wrecks and spare parts for those vehicles. At the time, I had no garage or place to leave my tools out and—paying alimony on one marriage and supporting another—hadn't felt that I could afford a truck. My pal Dave Butler, the founder of VPW, assured me I could and that he would make it happen (and did). On my first visit there, we went for coffee in town, and I was surprised at the excellence of my cappuccino. (I had gone to school in Iowa for four years in the sixties and could never have previously conceived that I would ever get a cappuccino, let alone an excellent one, in Iowa.)

Dave and I were sitting at an outside table when three friends of his approached and sat down with us. They were exceedingly nice people—open and "on the one," an old be-bop expression meaning "in the moment." Normally, when meeting new people, I'm on alert because my status as a movie actor often generates projections, and people are sometimes overly deferential or too aggressive, as if they believe I think I'm something special. None of these people behaved that way, and it was surprising to meet three strangers with whom no projections arose.

The next morning, we went for coffee again, and three new people joined us, and they were the same type of folks—open, good-humored, relaxed, and in the moment. I didn't say anything, but neither did the coincidence escape me.

By the end of the third morning, with three new, equally refined and enjoyable folks, I turned to Dave after they left and said, "Dave, color me stupid, but something's going on here." And I recounted my feelings about the people we'd met.

He laughed and informed me that in 1973 the Maharishi Mahesh Yogi and his followers had come to Fairfield and bought Parsons College, turning it into Maharishi International University, whose curriculum was organized around meditation. Dave and his friends had all been students and then faculty and then had tired of the bureaucratic entanglements of a large institution and had left but remained in Fairfield and established their lives.

I was embarrassed at myself. I had always looked down my snobby Zen nose at the Maharishi, guru of the Beatles, as a lightweight. What did he know compared to my long, imaginary lineage of Zen samurai and adepts? I had to admit that these folks were the peers of many of my old Zen comrades, and I decided, then and there, that the technology of meditation itself is the technology affecting deep change. I was not deterred in my commitment to Buddhism, but I was forced to drop my prejudicial judgments about other forms of practice.

So let's discuss meditation.

MEDITATION

Zazen is the general term for Zen meditation. *Shikantaza* is a form of meditation associated with the Japanese Soto Zen School. It does not require focused attention on anything, such as counting the breath, but is "just sitting." When we meditate and follow our breathing—with the body still, the spine erect, and the back of one hand resting in the palm of another, thumbs lightly touching—not only is the mind deprived of extraneous stimulation and engagement but a portion of our awareness is also sequestered, dedicated to our awareness of breath, posture, and *mudra* (hand position). The hand position helps to keep the meditator present: should the thumbs separate or the circle collapse, the meditator realizes that his or her attention to body and posture has lapsed and can correct it.

It is this sequestration that offers awareness a stable perch from which to regard thoughts and impulses of the mind and body without being seized and distracted by them. We are not texting, listening to music, watching the news, making to-do lists, or dedicating ourselves to any self-organized purpose at all. Neither are we trying to inculcate any specific state of mind. Rather, we sit in our actual life in that moment as it is and pay attention to the full experience of being alive.

The first surprise for most beginners (and often used as an excuse for why they cannot meditate) is the busy-ness of the mind. It can feel like a conveyor belt dragging the observer from thought to thought, perception to perception, and scenario to scenario: things to be done, problems at home, daydreams and fantasies—the mind like a matador's red cape snaring the bull's attention. Because too many people believe that the purpose of meditation is to silence the mind, they struggle against the mind stream until they become exhausted. It's like trying to fight the tides. Poet and Zen adept Gary Snyder once observed that "the mind is a gland for producing images" and neither the content nor the endless succession of the images should be a problem. The problem is that *our attention is seduced by these images,* ensnared into committing to mental realms and beliefs that lead to impulsive action.

Deprived of stimuli, the mind begins to slow and soften *on its own accord.* Attempting to quiet one's mind creates an immediate dichotomy—one's idea of oneself and one's idea of mind. My lineage founder Shunryu Suzuki-roshi once cautioned a student who had appeared before him in a very self-congratulatory manner, declaring how "good" his zazen had become, saying, "*You* do not sit zazen. Zazen sits zazen."

While sitting, hearing may become more prominent and physical sensations (not always pleasant) emerge to the fore, anchoring the meditator firmly in the body. From this vantage point, the meditator observes his or her mind and body without distraction or interruption. This increased intimacy is the beginning of training the body to be tranquil and the mind to remain composed in the face of whatever thoughts, images, impulses, or discomforts that might arise. It is also an opportunity to review old narratives and beliefs.

The antidote to being dragged along by the conveyor belt of our thoughts is to settle into the body, mind, and breath. It is an always available keel for keeping us upright. As we sit, gradually extending mind over our entire breath and body, distinctions between body and mind dissolve.

As we become more practiced, it becomes easier to regard awareness like the blank screen in a movie theater. Because we know a movie is a projection, we can observe whatever occurs on the screen without undue distress. Similarly, we can begin to observe the thoughts generated by our brain as images projected on the screen of our awareness, making it easier to remain present, without flinching or distracting our-selves, even when difficult thoughts and feelings arise. Our awareness, like the blank movie screen, remains luminous, calm, and able to accept whatever arises. Even when we are angry or emotional, the awareness itself remains unruffled.

Meditating regularly will calm body and mind and aid the set-tling into your life. "To settle" does not mean to uncritically agree with every event. It means to acknowledge them without delusion. Whatever exists, exists because of previous circumstances. It arrives on its own trajectories from its own historical continuity, with its own legitimacy, whether or not we approve or disapprove. That is the Big Mind perspec-tive. Big Mind is the formless common denominator of reality before subdivision by language and concepts into contradictory opposites.

From the point of view of our singular existence, however, and par-ticularly our vows as Buddhists, acknowledging everything does not mean tolerating everything, in the sense that we would remain neutral about all events and acts. Thich Nhat Hanh, the Vietnamese Zen mas-ter, was on everyone's death list during the war for his resistance efforts, but he resisted as a Buddhist—raising awareness, witnessing, certifying by his presence. Threats to other beings, to the environment, threats to compassion and the requirements of life must be acknowledged and resisted if we are to honor our vows. It would probably not involve kill-ing but might definitely involve self-sacrifice.

Resistance does not mean hating those you oppose or using an "issue" as the occasion to project violence and hostility on others. Clarity will make it clear that both opponents are parts of a much larger field, and it is delusional to consider ourselves "good" and our opponent "evil." Buddhists disapprove of the action, not the actor. The actors are not permanently consigned to reproduce negative behavior forever. Anyone can awaken from the slumber of considering themselves sepa-rate from the universe. Consequently, Buddhists try not to blame others or generate anger and revilement but place their own bodies at sites of critical danger or violence to interdict. They bear witness, meditating

Vietnamese Mahayana Buddhist monk Thich Quang Duc
burns himself to death at a busy intersection in Saigon
(photo credit: Malcolm Browne)

or modeling nonviolent behavior and staying true to the Buddha's edict
to do no harm.

Those who consider such witnessing ineffective should consider the
example of Thich Quang Duc, a Vietnamese Buddhist monk who, in
June of 1963, as a protest against the Vietnamese government's perse-
cution of Buddhists, burned himself alive on a busy street surrounded
by 350 fellow monks bearing witness. He remained sitting upright in
a perfect zazen posture until he keeled over, at which point he righted
himself and resumed his formal posture until he died.

David Halberstam, reporter for the *New York Times,* was there and
described the event.

> I was to see that sight again, but once was enough. Flames were com-
> ing from a human being; his body was slowly withering and shrivel-
> ing up, his head blackening and charring. In the air was the smell

of burning human flesh; human beings burn surprisingly quickly. Behind me I could hear the sobbing of the Vietnamese who were now gathering. I was too shocked to cry, too confused to take notes or ask questions, too bewildered to even think. . . . As he burned, he never moved a muscle, never uttered a sound, his outward composure in sharp contrast to the wailing people around him.[1]

In reference to the photograph of Quang Duc, President John F. Kennedy said: "No news picture in history has generated so much emotion around the world as that one." Most political observers believe that this photo created a turning point in the war and accelerated the demise of President Diem, for whom Quang Duc left the following note, remarkable for its gentleness, particularly in the face of the suffering he accepted for himself.

Before closing my eyes and moving toward the vision of the Buddha, I respectfully plead to President Ngo Dinh Diem to take a mind of compassion toward the people of the nation and implement religious equality to maintain the strength of the homeland eternally. I call the venerables, reverends, members of the sangha and the lay Buddhists to organize in solidarity to make sacrifices to protect Buddhism.[2]

He did not shout invective or urge violence. He sacrificed his own life to exemplify his commitment to ending the suffering of others and did it in a way that exemplified his Buddhist values. Simultaneously, he offered the world a galvanizing image of the suffering his people were undergoing not only from President Diem but from all parties creating the war. He achieved this through perfect meditation. This cannot be confused with "acceptance."

This photo and consideration of Thich Quang Duc offers us insight into just how fully the simple act of meditation can be an agent of personal and social transformation. It can help us achieve the courage to state our positions unequivocally but nonviolently.

Relaxing, allowing each exhale to help us sink back into Big Mind is like remembering that you are both the ocean *and* the wave, allowing your awareness to settle in a place where separation between us and "the rest of it" no longer exists.

In the short term, meditation improves concentration, discipline, and steadiness because repeatedly recalling wayward attention back to the breath and body is like teaching a puppy to sit or mastering an instrument. Meditation bolsters one's courage to face internal and physical discomforts, and within a very few months, as the body develops strength and the mind develops discipline, one begins to experience a palpable, interior spaciousness, somewhat like reducing the pressure in a boiling pot by removing the lid. You'll find it easier to acknowledge people and events as they are, as opposed to how you want them to be, and consequently find it easier to connect fearlessly to others, without the necessity of trying to alter them or situations to your liking.

I was in my late thirties when I discovered this. Like all knowledge it arrived with a headiness that generated enthusiasm and dedication. At the same time, however, there was something uncannily familiar about aspects of Zen practice, and it took me a decade more of practice to discover what it was. The familiarity was resident in my work as an actor. I began working with young students, teaching acting classes, first at the San Francisco Zen Center and then at other zen groups, pursuing clarity about the connections I felt between Zen practice and acting. The catalyst for my understanding came from my experiences with masks.

The mask encounters are an easier, less-disciplined, and predictably more amusing way to meet the subject of no fixed self: a risk-free, pain-free introduction to ego-diminished states of mind. We return from such encounters refreshed by having highlighted previously invisible aspects of ourselves, and with those revelations arrive expanded options and possibilities. Remembering that cemented the possibility of using masks as an adjunct to Zen practice and teaching.

🔯 🔯 🔯

3
Working with Masks

Mask work is a powerful means for tapping into character. In the mask workshop, I met Marla and Veronica, two characters unlike me and unlike each other. I felt I knew them, but they were also revealing themselves to me as we worked.

AMY LARSON, WORKSHOP PARTICIPANT

Upon donning the mask, the self evaporates, and one becomes a tabula rasa, an "original face"—both nothing and potentially anything—forging ahead in the moment on gut instincts, along with a beginner mind's sense of curiosity and exploration.

SEAN CAIN, WORKSHOP PARTICIPANT

Without some training, simply placing a mask over your face and looking in a mirror may paralyze rather than liberate your imagination. Occasionally, the experience of disappearing proves unsettling to some. One night a seasoned Zen student was visiting and insisted on trying on a mask, despite having done no warm-ups or preparations. I was curious to see what might occur and agreed.

When he encountered his masked reflection, he became emotionally frozen. He could *describe* what he felt arising from the mirror, but some emotional detachment prevented him from expressing his feelings as *behavior.* He could not integrate new impulses into his body or psyche in any way, nor could he express any *intention.* The self is a strict master and has to be either exhausted or seduced to let go.

Richard Baker-roshi, first abbot of the San Francisco Zen Center after Shunryu Suzuki's death in 1971, once observed during a lecture that "the body is the unconscious. We store things in there—in the muscles and ligaments—that are too important to forget." Old psychic wounds and impressions, once too important to forget, are deeply buried in our muscles and ligaments. Like landmines abandoned after a war, they remain hidden, their potential for damage undiminished by time. A psychiatrist once told me, "In the unconscious, it's always this morning." He meant that the unconscious has no sense of time; all its memories are pungent and immediate. However, even in the extreme case of my Zen friend, wearing a mask highlighted a path by identifying a problem he could not deny. Suffice it to say, since then, I have never shortchanged warm-up games and exercises. Consequently, I urge students (and readers) to be patient during descriptions of exercises, which may appear, at first blush, to have little or nothing to do with ego-less states.

Pointless or silly as they may appear, these games are not addressed to the intellect but to the *body* and *Big Mind,* the surrounding vastness in which all ideas about one's self float. Enlightenment is not something we *think* about but *express* in each moment. Each exercise is designed to alter some sense of the body's feelings about "normal" by coaxing you to imagine, move, stand, behave, and project yourself in ways that appear to you as counterintuitive and definitely *not-you.* These simple games expose the borders and soften the sense of self by encouraging you to explore attitudes, feelings, physical postures, intentions, and *behavior* beyond the safety of your known persona. If, for instance, you begin to move in a way that does not *feel* like you, it's possible to become fully aware of that resistance, identify it, and study it clearly rather than dismiss it or flee its influence. *Why* is it not you? What's wrong with it, other than your discomfort?

Richard Baker-roshi, the abbot at the San Francisco Zen Center when I began my practice there, once asked me to attend a function with him. I knew I would encounter people there I did not like, and so I demurred, saying that I would be uncomfortable in that situation. His immediate response was, "What's wrong with being uncomfortable?" His answer indicated a door for me to consider passing through. Who had made that decision, and why had my discomfort been suddenly elevated to the highest priority?

If your normal posture and social strategies represent a desire not to be noticed, being compelled to behave boldly or aggressively will awaken a host of resistances, worries, and previously rejected feelings. If you fear that spontaneous responses might expose you as foolish and reveal unconscious baggage or if being out-of-control frightens you, these exercises will have revelatory value. They may initially feel off-task or trivial, but they're extremely practical for highlighting aspects of the self normally consigned to invisibility.

The more familiar you are with your habits and partialities, the more easily you can alter them. These exercises address the unconscious directly, feeding it new information and strange associations, which nudge it off balance and onto high alert. It is that high-alert state seeking normalcy that, when presented with an unknown mask, scrambles to assemble a new, coherent personality that matches associations with the face in the mirror.

After a morning's exercises and games (which will be detailed later), the masks are introduced. The masks are *neutral* masks that do not express any particular emotion. However, there is a definite *quality* to their neutrality, a tabula rasa that allows maximal space for the wearer (and audience) to read qualities into the strange face. This blankness makes them mutable; each person's body and head shape alters the mask's emotional tone. A neutral mask may appear docile and defeated on one person, edgy and sullen on another, and seductive or provocative on a third. It is the mask's emptiness or lack of qualities that facilitates these transformations. Some masks work, and others do not, and it's hard to determine which will work at first look. One of my favorite masks is a stamped, nearly featureless plastic face that cost a dollar. It has enormous eye holes but somehow always transforms the wearer by bringing forth a very clear personality. (You can see that mask in the mirror on page 24.)

For Buddhists, it is the emptiness (formlessness) at the root of all things that generates the world's infinite variety of forms. If emptiness had any fixed qualities, there would be things it could not express. In mask work, that emptiness is the vacuum the mind abhors and rushes to fill in with data.

Class always opens with some minutes of meditation. After that, the better part of the morning session is dedicated to exercises and games. When it feels right, we meet the masks. Students are called up in groups of three to five. They are instructed to turn their backs to the class, and I stand before them holding an eighteen-inch-square mirror close to their faces. As they slip on a mask and arrange their hair over its edges I encourage them to alter the angle of their head—tilting one way or another, looking up from under their brows or down their nose, widening or narrowing their eyes, regarding the mirror directly or obliquely—until something clicks. When that occurs for them, they nod to indicate that they've got it. I remind them that if they begin to lose the new identity they must simply call out "mirror," and I'll return so they can reconnect to it.

When you see a mask as your reflection, several things occur simultaneously. A face, which is not your own, offers feedback to the mind. Seeking order and coherence, the mind mines its resources, scavenging clues, such as previously stored images from fantasies and dreams, to reestablish a new equilibrium. From that plunge into interior space, awareness rag-picks among random memories, feelings, observations, and emotions to assemble a holographic new personality. The new identity is as multidimensional as the old and will include knowledge of the masked persona's personal history, relatives, posture, attitudes toward the world, and pungent biographical details. It is as if everything you know about

Meeting the new self (author's collection)

yourself transformed into a door through which to discover someone else.

While your familiar identity remains in suspension, it will not trip you up with judgments, criticism, self-consciousness, and embarrassment. All its constituent parts that normally cause you difficulty are subdued. This occurs in the blink of an eye, and to anyone who has ever experienced the shock of recognition of a new character arising in their interior, it feels miraculous, as if that person had always been resident in your shadows, like an understudy waiting their opportunity to claim the stage.

Masks obliterate the gap between the self and the self that watches the self by temporarily repressing the ego. What's key is that our attachment to our own identity is sufficiently softened so that the mask is able to redirect previously dedicated energy into the new identity.

Because of the playful context and because the self has been "messed with" in a convivial, risk-free environment, masks displace normal fears of surrender that might accompany losing our grip in front of strangers. This softened attachment allows us to slip the ego's dominance temporarily, and our escape also releases us from our personality's historical problems. The startling and novel feedback of an unrecognizable face in the mirror offers consciousness new data points on which to fix its predictive functions. This new face provokes new associations, which are absorbed into the trance state, induced by the mask. Modern brain research has learned that, in the interests of efficiency, the mind makes rapid predictions as to what it may be observing, based on small amounts of data. The efficiency of this predictive function allows rapid decision-making to occur without exhaustive analysis of *all* data points.

The mask's persona perceives differently than "you" do and seizes possibilities that our ordinary self has excluded from its options. The masked persona responds to challenges or surprises with aplomb and rises to unexpected questions without hesitation or embarrassment and usually with glee and a pronounced attitude. The responses are ego-free or, more accurately, represent the ego of the mask, not your own. Furthermore, no matter how diffidently or unsure students may have been at the beginning of class, once masked, they stand before their peers as radically different people. Some will be insanely aggressive, others smoldering and cocksure; some will be barking mad, others perfectly normal. But always the student becomes someone different from the person he or she was at the beginning of class.

Masks are doorways into altered states, and in those states, the rigid boundaries of our old identity become permeable. To give ourselves permission to enter such states, we may need to face fears that losing control might expose us in some embarrassing manner or stain our reputations. Avoiding such thought-traps is exactly why we wear masks! We may often censor behavior, but we needn't censor our imaginations, and in a mask, the imagination is given free rein.

With their new identities secured, players turn around to face the class. I conduct short interviews with each as an introduction to the class. Invariably, these new personalities appear fully formed, completely conversant with facts about their family history, siblings, biographies of parents, and reasons for being there, which, moments earlier, did not exist. Their attitudes are markedly different, and their sense of improvisation markedly more committed and skillful. The delineations of character are very clear, and mask wearers are often surprised to find themselves funnier, sharper, and more intelligent or responsive than they were before putting on the mask.

Shy students sometimes become edgy and aggressive, claiming space and dominance in ways that would have been unthinkable to them earlier. Elderly women become cheerleaders or sirens; overweight young men prance about with narcissistic abandon, considering themselves irresistible. It is an astonishing thing to witness, as if a room full of people had been simultaneously seized with an impulse to drop all social facades and affectations and reveal who they truly are. The closest thing I can recall to witnessing such an experience is the memory of walking down Haight Street, San Francisco, in 1967 at the crazy height of the counterculture.

People who, at the beginning of class, labored to be diligent and correct, intelligent and well mannered, have been replaced by public fumblers, aggressive grifters, sexually voracious or viciously dictatorial women, satyrs, weeping confessors, and . . . *they are all wondrous!* That's the inexplicable truth. Each possesses an undeniable suchness that is so bald, candid, and indisputably authentic that they are impossible to ignore, judge, or dismiss.

Sometimes newly masked students are reduced to guttural utterances. Some masks need to learn to speak, while others have their own, fully formed languages, dialects, and accents. Relieved of the self's familiar shoulds and shouldn'ts, many revert to a primal level of childhood: stealing, being sly and mischievous, regarding the simplest articles—a red ball, a dog toy—as if they were miraculously assembled before their eyes, experiencing much the same sense of freshened curiosity one experiences on a psychedelic trip.

When the students' new personalities have jelled and they have been interacting in character for a while, the first three are asked to stand before the group, remove and hold their masks against their stomachs (always interesting because the old and new selves are simultaneously on display), answer class questions, and relate their experience behind the mask. After everyone in the class has had a turn, we begin another round. People are introduced to new masked characters in groups of

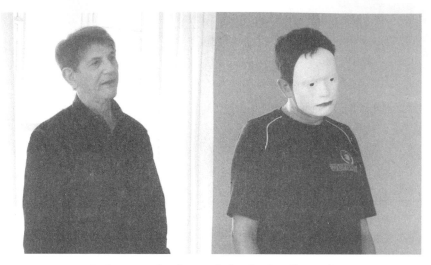

Taken over by the mask (author's collection)

three, and the process begins again. No one fully understands *how* they know who they are or how they answer questions and respond with such certainty, but players learn to trust their intuitive responses, and more often than not, their responses are startling and fresh. By the time everyone has experienced three masks, we can begin to discuss the relationship of these experiences to *their* ideas of whom or what their self is, and at this point I introduce the Buddhist perspective on the self.

During the 1960s I had an African American friend named John Francis who traveled the entire country carrying a banjo and never speaking. He could neither explain himself nor ask directly for anything, but he occasionally resorted to writing notes. Yet, he was so tuned by silence that this tall, singular black man was able to travel wherever he chose and, to my knowledge, never experienced any negative reaction. By choosing not to speak, he enhanced his hearing and general awareness, like a blind person. It is not that blind people, as a class, hear better but that, in the absence of sight, they have been forced to become more intimate with their remaining senses. This next exercise serves us in the same manner. It's very simple.

Imagine your face as a mask that cannot speak. (Some people discover exactly such a condition when they first don a mask.) A mask that cannot speak does not attach itself too literally to thoughts and concepts because it must communicate with the entire body. This is a second order of knowing, much like how a dancer communicates, which brings its own rewards as an additional mode of expression.

Extend the exercise by regarding the faces of people you pass in the streets as masks, and you'll be startled to discover archetypical visages reappearing in the world, defying all edicts of political correctness—greedy faces, evil faces, sullen faces, sad faces, bemused faces, not-nice faces—and translucent to the dominant emotions behind them.

A PARABLE

Buddha watched the two men approaching. He noticed their collapsed posture and frayed clothes, noticed too that the large white horse was lame in its right front foot and that both steeds were deeply tired and underfed. He imagined and then materialized a bucket, walked to the spring, and filled it with fresh water. He imagined and materialized a long cutting blade like he'd used when he was young in Nepal and collected a goodly pile of grass. Then he blew the coals of his fire into flame and set the tea kettle on to boil. As the strangers approached, he stepped forward without hesitation. "Let me take your horses."

The Lone Ranger thanked him and dismounted stiffly. Tonto noted the stranger's dark skin and bare feet, the tidiness and meagerness of his camp. "We can't stay here long," he whispered to the Lone Ranger. "He's got less than we do."

The Lone Ranger corrected him in a whisper: "If he's a fan, our visit will be enormously important to him."

"Sure, we'll eat his food and bury him in our importance," Tonto muttered to himself.

The Buddha indicated several soft pillows, which the strangers hadn't previously noticed, and invited them to make themselves comfortable.

While they settled, Buddha stripped the saddles and turned them upside down to dry in the sun. He flipped the saddle blankets and hung them over cottonwood branches to air out. He gave each horse a bucket of water and gently examined their feet and legs. Finding a stone in Silver's right front foot, he pried it clear of the hoof with a stick. Silver nudged him with his head, and the Buddha said, "You're welcome."

The Buddha returned to the fire, poured the tea, and set some naan bread before them, spiced with wild onions and some toasted peppers. The Lone Ranger ate his greedily. Tonto ate slowly, sampling and enjoying the strange flatbread. "I could teach this guy to make fry bread," he thought.

The Lone Ranger, like you and me, has accepted and then nurtured a fixed set of ideas concerning his identity. Being raised white in a white-majority culture, he has learned a sense of entitlement and superiority, which leaks from him, despite his goodwill and good intentions. It is an incontrovertible consequence of having been initiated into the world-view of his parents and society before having had the opportunity to decide such matters for himself. Such attitudes and beliefs are imbibed with mother's milk by those who identify or can be identified as "white" in this culture. They do not have to remain permanent, however.

The Lone Ranger's basically unconscious identity selects his feelings and perceptions and filters them through received and learned filters. Like Facebook, reality gives the impression of simply being discovered, when in reality sophisticated algorithms have previously determined what Facebook places before your awareness and what it doesn't—allowing the viewer to assume that "that's the way things are." This sense of freedom is illusory, and rather than being as free as the Lone Ranger (or we may believe he is), we are obligated to follow the edicts of our intangible, invisible self, which rules us with an iron hand. The primary secret it keeps from us is that we are not bound to follow its edicts and there is a larger, vaster reality beyond its perimeters.

⚐ ⚐ ⚐

4

Just Who Do You Think You Are?

This was the most vexing question demanded of me as a child by my parents when I had done something to displease them. It was simultaneously a demotion of status, an accusation of transgression, and an existentially paralyzing question because it was unanswerable. How could I possibly express all the selves whirling around inside me in a single declaration? I was too young to understand the enormous potential of this inability to answer and so usually stood mute and ashamed, while my irked parent informed me very clearly who "I" was.

At the root of most personal problems is our *idea* of who we are and our belief that despite some change it remains primarily fixed while it is the world outside us that changes constantly. That idea represents a minute fraction of what we actually are, but it normally serves us due to its efficiency and conservation of energy in solving quotidian problems. Achieving real intimacy with our ideas of who we are can be an important part of correcting problems we associate with ourselves. *Who* is having them? *Who* is perceiving them? Why do so many personal dilemmas appear to be repetitive?

There's a teaching parable about a man walking down a darkened street one night who falls into a deep hole. He is outraged that there were no warning lights or sawhorses delineating its edges, no yellow tape blocking his path. Furious, he clambers out and goes home.

The next night he is traveling the same road and falls into the hole again. He is even more irate this night, exclaiming: "This hole has been here for over twenty-four hours and no one has done anything!" he fumes. "It's completely irresponsible." He resolves to call the mayor and the highway department. He struggles out and returns home.

The third night he falls in again, only this time he berates himself. "What's the matter with me? This is the third time this has happened. I knew it was here, and I did it anyway. Am I stupid? Why can't I learn?"

The fourth night, he takes a different street.

This is how we all learn. This is why Buddhists refer to mindfulness and our dedication to following the Eightfold Path as a practice.

How do we get a bead on the thinker whom we imagine is distracting us and generating our troublesome thoughts and feelings? How do we isolate this "self" from the erratic impulses and sensations coursing through our mind stream like the steel ball in a pinball machine? Suppose we were to determine that there was no fixed self in there, simply awareness forwarding information to us from a number of receptors simultaneously, with consciousness offering us the overview? If you were to experience something like this, would you consider that it might be possible that such a change of perception could change your relationship to those problems, that even if the problem continued to exist, you might not identify with it in quite the same way or be as stymied by it?

One of the most reliable ways to catch glimpses of how we think about our self occurs when we're called on to do something novel, perhaps scary, or uncomfortable. In such a moment, an impulse—perhaps shyness, aversion, or anxiety—intercedes, informing us that *this is not me.* Because it is our own thought, in our own familiar voice, we tend to trust it, again, as we trust Facebook—as an objective discovery requiring no further examination. By doing that, we surrender our autonomy to our habits and ideas whether or not they are false or serve us.

Developing our tolerance for anxiety and uncertainty and the patience to resist snap judgments can highlight these normally invisible judgments and decisions.

These "edges" of the self, highlighted by discomfort, embarrassment, fear of the unknown, or resistance, are a direct lens through which to view our identity. This is not to challenge ethical decisions we've arrived at as conscious adults but to tease out normally invisible opinions and decisions we have accepted or implied about ourselves without being aware of them.

HIDING THE SELF BEHIND MASKS

Readers may associate masks with Halloween, grand balls, and outlaws, but after more than forty years of Zen practice and life as a professional actor and after experimenting and teaching mask workshops for much of that time, I can assert that after only a few preliminary exercises *a mask will substitute its own personality for yours* while you wear it. Furthermore, that replacement delivers many of the positive, liberating effects of psychedelics but without any physical aftereffects. Masks so easily induce ego-suppressed states that I've nicknamed the phenomenon "enlightenment-lite." What both masks and psychedelics share is a temporary dethroning of the ego, nullifying its primacy and allowing the mind to assemble an altogether new self, which will direct the wearer with the same authority as the one you woke up with that morning. With the evaporation of the old persona, a sense of wholeness, marked diminishment of self-consciousness, second-guessing, and self-criticism emerge. Perhaps best of all, a feeling of merging with the creative energy flows of the larger universe is almost universally reported.

Obviously, I am asking readers to take this assertion on faith until they try it for themselves, and so throughout this book I've included testimonials from classes and workshops so that readers can learn the impressions of others who've previously done this work. Hopefully, these testimonials will inspire confidence and support the impulse to try mask work on your own.*

What connects these practices to meditating Buddhism and makes them mutually useful is that they are both related to a common experience of suppressing the ego, an appetizer for the main course in the same way that mystical experiences while meditating are not "the goal" but markers to confirm that you're on the right route. Like children's play, mask games are rehearsals for life skills and the deeper wisdom available to us when we manage to put our small-mind self on hold and get out of our own way. The fact that we can enter such territory through fun and games is the same order of inducement flowers offer to bees.

A caution is in order: if one begins the search for enlightenment as somehow in a different geographical location or state of mind than your ordinary life, it doesn't work. Thinking about enlightenment as a concrete, graspable, permanent state of mind creates, by implication, a polarizing condition—an imagined "you" who resides in one place imagining "enlightenment" existing in another. Mark my words, the twain will never meet. The temporary states produced by drugs and masks offer tasty appetizers to the main dish—release and sense of union—but they are not the meal itself. To eat at this table, one must "sit," and what Buddhists refer to as sitting is meditation. It is finally, through meditation, the unconditional, undistracted intimacy with the mind that understanding and acceptance of what we really are becomes clear to us.

A PARABLE

The sun was a palm's width above the eastern horizon when the Lone Ranger woke from fifteen hours of dead sleep. When his eyes opened,

---

*Readers interested in mask work can reach me at petercoyote.com or at peter@wdprod .com for details.

he slid surreptitiously out of his bedroll to check his saddlebags. His stash of silver bullets was still there, wrapped in an old bandanna, and the gold coins as well. He wandered into camp to find the Buddha brushing Silver with a stiff brush fixed to his hand with a rubber strap. "I wonder where'n the hell he had that stashed," the Lone Ranger thought. "Maybe we can bargain for it when we leave, or I'll ask for it as a parting gift. He doesn't have horses."

Silver's right front fetlock and ankle had been freshly wrapped in soft cloth over what appeared to be a layer of freshly crushed leaves. The Buddha noticed him observing it and said, as if he'd heard a question, "Comfrey. It'll help the swelling and soreness."

The Lone Ranger noticed that the strange little man had brushed Tonto's pony, Scout, first, because his coat gleamed, and all the snarls and burrs had been removed from his tail and mane. Both horses had been washed. Silver stood dreamily content, his lower lip comically relaxed, while Buddy-Boy (or whatever his name was) combed away months of dirt and tangle. The Lone Ranger decided to bide his time about correcting him on the protocol error of failing to notice the difference between master and servant. He could understand how a dark-skinned foreigner might not have noticed that Tonto was not a white man because he wasn't either. However, that did not excuse the fact that Tonto's horse should always be attended after the Ranger's. He would save that perhaps as a gentle rebuke to the stranger's master to demonstrate that, as two men of property and power, they understood these things. Who knows, it might give the Lone Ranger a little edge in negotiating a loan. The Lone Ranger would be gentle in explaining the transgression because Buddy-Boy had been exemplary—all service and speaking mostly only when spoken to, but still, the little things were important.

With the horses cared for, Buddha inquired, "Could you eat?"

"I could eat a horse," the Lone Ranger said. Tonto looked at him like he was an idiot and then checked Buddha's reaction. Buddha smiled as if the Lone Ranger had made a joke and, nodding to include

Tonto, responded, "I'm a vegetarian, but I'll whip something up."

He disappeared behind the huge boulder and returned with some large and small sacks and began preparing a pot of lentils spiced with wild onions, sage, cumin, and allspice. The scent was overpoweringly delicious to the hungry visitors. He dumped some flour into a pot, stirred it with a bit of water, added some chia seeds, formed the dough into slabs, and began to cook naan bread on a large flat rock he had been heating near the fire.

The Lone Ranger, noticing the appearance of so many foodstuffs, rose casually, stretched, and announced in an idle voice, "I'm going to relieve myself." He slipped around the boulder, furtively seeking what he imagined would be vast stores that could be bargained for or "borrowed" to aid their return journey to Hollywood. He was perturbed to notice that there was nothing there, only undisturbed sand. He peeked under every rock, in every crevice. Nothing. "That old boy is shrewder than he looks," he thought. "I'm gonna have to keep an eye on him."

He ambled back to the fire to find Tonto scooping lentils out of a bowl and explaining to their host, "All we've eaten for months is hardtack and jerky. This is a lifesaver."

The Lone Ranger felt a flush of anger at the ingratitude. All the work he'd given Tonto in LA, and now at the first hard patch, he's bitching in front of a stranger about the food. The Lone Ranger sat down stiffly, and Buddha handed him a bowl. After sampling it, he involuntarily found himself gulping down the savory bean stew the Buddha had prepared for their bodies.

Despite their contributions to understanding how formless the self actually is, both psychedelics and masks share common drawbacks. Primary among them are that both experiences of liberation are finite and can't be regenerated continually in daily life without recourse to another mask or more drugs. Both may precipitate changes and insights, which can linger and inform future life to some degree. Both offer a heightened sense of freedom and appreciation of the aliveness of the world. Both may radically alter your vistas and perspective. However, with no negative connotation intended, both are crutches. If an experience cannot be replicated without the masks or drug, the illuminations are as dependent on them as a man with a bad knee is on his cane. Furthermore, without the constant rededication of mindfulness and practice, your old habits will soon regain supremacy and enmesh you firmly back in your old "normal."

My final Buddhist teacher, Lewis Richmond, once described a psychedelic trip as like "being flown to the Grand Canyon in a helicopter." The vista, scale, and beauty are breathtaking and jar the mind out of its complacency and normal egocentricity. But when your trip comes to an end, you're unable to find your way back because you were transported by helicopter. You never mapped the journey and followed the path with your own resources and efforts.

No one would assert that such a trip is without merit, but a trip to the Grand Canyon may not help a traveler who struggles with deep issues of shame, anger, or envy. The trip may displace those feelings temporarily, but because they are deeply engrained in the body-mind continuum, great persistence is required to alter them permanently. Awesome as psychedelics may be, they do not necessarily instill discipline, diligence, fixed intention to change, compassion, equanimity, or intuition.

I have friends who travel regularly to Peru to ingest ayahuasca with shamans. I know others who take microdoses of LSD, attempting to foster creativity at the office. Still others are taking advantage of the legality of pot in California to stay stoned. All appreciate the freedom of being "off the hook" and the rapture of their illuminated experiences, and aside from some risk to those whose identities may be precarious, I see nothing wrong with experimenting with psychedelics as long as one realizes they are not the kensho experience one receives cold sober through meditation. Neither are they the calm appreciation of "things as they are," unadorned by description, concepts, and ideas. I've had LSD trips that were twelve hours of ecstasy and spent others backed into a corner battling my demons. Everything has a shadow, and until we wake up to the fact that *the ordinary itself is miraculous,* we remain hooked on intriguing thoughts and concepts that may entertain but invariably disappoint us.

Drug experiences do not enhance skills to disengage from our thoughts and unruly emotions or discipline our impulses. Drugs may buffer the difficulties and discomforts that arise in daily life, but they do not teach us the fortitude, patience, and resolve to get through bad patches by our own devices. Masks offer a flash of expansion, illumination, and usually joy, which has a kinship to meditative states—certainly enough to whet one's appetite for deeper exploration. The deeper exploration I hope to interest you in is meditation and understanding Buddhist thought.

Transcendental states require sustained engagement of will and intention to succeed. Personal experience has convinced me that when these states are generated through your own efforts, *without* drugs, your confidence that a permanent transformation has happened will be higher—versus the transient nature of chemically induced states. The world is littered with the wreckage of psychedelic voyagers who left all the heavy lifting of change to chemistry. Neither drugs nor masks are particularly useful at *sustaining* ego-diminished states because they have done the work for us. The real trick, which meditation delivers, involves sustaining a vision of the ordinary, even the parts you don't like, as miraculous expressions of emptiness, unrepeatable expressions of the universe.

If you stop to think about it, the existence of a housefly and all its attendant realities is an unfathomable mystery. Why has the universe chosen to express itself in this way? It is just as true for our own existence. There are many theories and ideas as to why and how life takes certain forms, but none of these approaches the magic of the thing itself. Any life-form or object can provide the path that returns us to the Grand Canyon. You should understand that the path requires nothing more than our own energy to follow it.

Should you eventually accept the lessons of your masked experience and the Buddha's teaching that the self is not a fixed entity, it is a short step to conclude that *numerous configurations of one's self are available.* We are not permanently stained by previous errors and acts, limiting beliefs, counterproductive habits, bad deeds, and misunderstandings. Neither are we ever permanently elevated to some imagined perfection of understanding and wisdom. A Zen master who is not paying attention is no different from any other absentminded person. It is our common delusion, our belief in a fixed and unchangeable entity that condemns us to our habitual reality and generates *dukkha.*

In a mask workshop you'll discover new identities that fit as snugly as the old. When you change masks, you'll discover others that fit equally well. By the workshop's end, having inhabited two or three very different but complete personas, you will have certified for yourself that the entity you once regarded as your unalterable self is as fluid as water or a gas. You'll have experienced a visceral prelude of the freedom that meditation affords. For many of my students, these masked states have served as an inducement to explore meditation. Nothing in you is fixed but your habits, intentions, and assumptions, and even they are ungraspable. If you should develop an interest in practicing meditation (for which you'll receive instruction later in this book), you'll eventually understand that the face you entered the room with is also a mask—sometimes useful, sometimes not—but the choice of when and how you use that knowledge will, from that time forward, be under your authority.

Buddha worked his way to a deep understanding of why and how humans create needless suffering. Everything he taught can be confirmed or denied through your own experience, not written texts or hand-me-down verities. We do not worship Buddha as a god because his status as a human is unchallenged. Much of what appears to be worship is actually formal expressions of gratitude for his teaching, but at the end of the day, Buddha is your own innate wisdom. You don't have to abandon any religion to take advantage of his teaching. I can say with confidence that there is no conflict between the practice of Buddhism and any particular religious practice (except perhaps cannibalism).

A PARABLE

The next morning, refreshed by a good night's sleep, cradled by the sand, they woke to savory cups of herbal tea. Tonto noticed approvingly that their horses were eating piles of what looked like hay. He hadn't noticed much grass around during the past few days and was curious as to how this sprightly stranger had managed to gather so much.

The Buddha returned and lifted a cloth off a bowl filled with thick slices of yeastless bread, which he set before them, along with a pot of wild honey.

"You don't travel light," Tonto observed.

"None of this weighs a thing," the Buddha answered smiling mysteriously. "It's empty."

The Lone Ranger pulled a silver pocket watch out of his pocket and checked the time, as if the stopped watch had been wound and he had somewhere else to be. The Buddha noticed. "Did the heart arrive?" he inquired straight-faced. The Lone Ranger had no idea what he was talking about.

Tonto caught the humorous edge of the remark and struggled not to laugh.

The Lone Ranger answered seriously: "My time is not my own." He scanned the horizon, turning his heroic profile slowly from left to right, as he always did to give people the opportunity to look at him. (He'd learned that trick from Cary Grant.)

"Whose is it then?" Buddha asked.

"My life is dedicated to good works and the elimination of evil," the Lone Ranger answered, in the deep and mellifluous voice that had inspired audiences of thousands.

Buddha appeared surprised. "Good Lord," he said and looked at Tonto inquisitively. Tonto smiled wanly and shrugged.

The Lone Ranger has a plan to return to Hollywood and refresh his career. He has no idea that times have changed and that "good guys in white hats" have been rendered passé by the horrors of multiple wars, 9/11, and the systemic betrayals of working people. Without questioning the validity of his goal (and who among us has not imitated him?), he begins strategizing how he will gain the means to achieve it, ignoring the magical Buddha right in front of him.

5

Tricking and Trapping the Self

"You're not who think you are" is what's stuck with me most since the class. I suppose you could rephrase that to "You're a hell of a lot more than you're aware of." There is something magical that occurs with the mask and the mirror—a gate opened to the subconscious and a welcome break from day-to-day self-critiques, limiting assessments, and various identity crises. It's a break I don't often realize is available. . . . Peter's emphasis here is valuable to any open-minded individual in any walk of life. . . . As adults, we've interacted with so many different people over the years—all impressing and accumulating some amount of human data into our minds. The mask work somehow summons characters from the stew . . . often with fantastic specificity. . . . Afterward, I felt much more balance, energy, optimism, and curiosity. I should really start meditating!

DAVID GAST, WORKSHOP PARTICIPANT

One of the enduring delights of working with students and masks is the unexpected breakthroughs and illuminations that rupture the surface of ordinary reality, like dolphins suddenly appearing above the ocean's surface. Many such experiences have certified for me how profound these practices can be and have bolstered my confidence to continue this practice for nearly forty-five years. My bias favors highlighting and improving Zen practice, but the same efficacy can occur with everyone—business executives to artists to electricians and politicians—anyone trying to access a more spacious and authentic understanding and the extraordinary problem-solving capacities of an unfettered mind.

Once, during a mask workshop for the Houston Zen Center, a woman student came to speak privately to me. She was an unusually large woman, large in every dimension, not fat but *big*—tall, broad hipped, and large breasted—and gave me the impression of holding reserves of physical power. However, in her interactions with others, she hunched her shoulders forward as if trying to diminish the prominence of her bosom and seemed to be attempting something similar with her personality, speaking softly and hesitantly, hyper alert, perhaps for the judgment of others.

After a morning dedicated to warm-up exercises and exploring the personal identifiers by which people know and express themselves, such as self-presentation, posture, intention, and a variety of games designed to illuminate habitually stuck areas, this woman remained diffident.

During the afternoon session, she donned a full-face mask and freed her hair to frame it. Studying her masked face in the mirror I held before her, she altered her posture, the angle of her head and eyes, trying on various gestures until something jelled, and a new, fully dimensional self arose unmistakably within her. It was startling.

Something "rode" her—a term Voodun practitioners use to describe the experience of being taken over by a spirit. It straightened her spine, and her body appeared to solidify, giving the impression of being unyielding. Her posture appeared solid as a standing boulder; her voice dropped into a lower, more commanding pitch and tone. The entire class was galvanized by her transfiguration and the indisputable power she radiated.

At one point in the class, two masked characters were improvising

Ghost Zen interview (author's collection)

a *dokusan*—the formal meeting between a Zen teacher and student. A "ghost" student was asking advice of a "ghost" Zen master played by this woman. Her responses were deep and insightful, arising out of some mysterious depth that had previously been smothered by her personality. When the session ended and the entire class burst into applause, she seemed stunned by the being she had discovered in her psyche.

The following year I returned to Houston for another class, and she signed up again. Chatting with her before we began, I asked her if she had retained anything of what she'd discovered the previous year. She laughed heartily and said, "Are you kidding me? After that class, I quit my job."

Anxious that the workshop might have "liberated" her into poverty, I asked her what she meant. "Well," she responded, "I didn't exactly quit. I walked into my boss's office and told him, 'I'm bored to death here, and I'm going to leave unless you can find me something interesting to do. Oh yes, *and* give me a substantial raise.'" Her boss must have been as shocked as I was because he complied with both requests. I was pleased to hear this but not overly surprised because witnessing profound changes in people wearing masks had ceased being unusual to me many years earlier.

That same year, during a different class at a Zen center in Austin, Texas, a short, wiry, rather plain woman with no makeup or adornments whatsoever, not even a ring, stepped forward. I guessed her to be in her midsixties, and her response to wearing a neutral mask was startling. The mask contributed a decidedly sexual aura to her, and on seeing herself in the mirror, she inhaled quickly and held her breath. She impulsively elongated her throat before the mirror and stroked it languidly for an instant, and then, as if she had received an electric shock, she wheeled away and began to hop and scamper around the room, squeaking like a monkey. I watched her, astonished, and then beckoned her over to ask about her behavior.

"I was making fun of the woman I saw," she said, as if it were a natural consequence.

"Why were you making fun of her?" I asked.

"Well," she paused for a long moment and then responded gravely, "she was too sexual."

I asked what "too sexual" meant, and she recounted a detailed and judgmental narrative about her mother's "misbehavior" with men, describing her as "a very sexy and seductive woman." As she related her tale, it became clear that her mother's behavior had precipitated some traumatic events during her childhood and that she remained pinioned in the grip of powerful emotions from that relationship. Her judgments were so inflexible that they prohibited her from even *playing* at sensuality, even protected by the anonymity of a mask. There was something tragic about her inability to coexist with her own sensuality.

Watching her psychic contortions reminded me of a book that had once impressed me—*The Drama of the Gifted Child* by Dr. Alice Miller. In that book, Dr. Miller asserts that gifted children are especially sensitive and responsive to their parents' wishes, even as infants. Should they express an emotion or behavior that offends their parents, the parents' displeasure is experienced by them as a withholding of love and care—abandonment—a traumatic event for a helpless baby.

This fear is so traumatic that the child intuitively censures the offending impulse from repetition. The unintended consequence of this decision is that the child has innocently banished a portion of his authenticity. The child is unable to understand that such a decision creates a double bind, which will haunt them through the rest of their life—the child's authenticity will always be at war with his need to be loved.

Vietnamese Zen master Thich Nhat Hanh identifies the fear of abandonment as the primal wound of humankind: "The memory of our helplessness as infants; our need for others to care for and protect us."

I felt my throat constrict with sadness watching this poor woman struggle to suppress the physical pleasure of having a body. Somewhere along the path of her life, she had conflated sensuality and sexuality with such powerful negative judgments that they were to be henceforth forbidden. I felt as if I was observing a life from which laughter had been condemned.

I am not a trained psychologist and am quite careful about specific advice to students that might impinge on territory best left to trained practitioners, because I've learned it's a mistake to believe that meditation will heal all wounds and confusion. It's been my experience that meditation and psychological therapy work extremely well together, and I often suggest that people seek a qualified therapist to help them with obdurate problems.

In this case, I suggested to her that she take a long and luxurious bath that evening. If she had candles, light them. If she had incense, light it. After relaxing in the tub—clean and refreshed, dried and comfortable—I suggested that she dress in her favorite clothes and jewelry and stand before a mirror. I told her that my hunch was that she would see not her mother but a very kind and lovely person enjoying the comforts of an indulgent bath and dressing up. I guaranteed that nothing that she perceived would harm her. I've not seen her since, but I sincerely hope that perhaps the mask's identifying her territory of psychic taboo offered her the incentive to explore and hopefully heal it.

By the time we become adults, most of us have learned to camouflage our most eccentric impulses and habits—usually those we feel to be most unique to ourselves, which might mark us as odd or strange to others. We assemble our faces and personalities into what we hope translates as the trustworthy "normal" person we would like to present to the world. Masks obliterate such strategies and open the sluices for previously checked impulses to flow freely.

Keith Johnstone, former director of improvisation at Britain's Royal Court Theatre, once told me how Charlie Chaplin had been unable to locate his signature character of the Little Tramp until he discovered the details of his "mask"—his quirky mustache and contradictory clothing of tight jacket, baggy pants, and cane. Every actor I've ever consulted about this subject has confirmed some similar experience concerning a character who may not have fully jelled for them until they were fully costumed and in makeup—masking their normal identity.

In his seminal and important book, *Impro*, Johnstone perfectly defines how masks function: *"A Mask is a device for driving the personality out of the body and allowing a spirit to take possession of it."*[1]

I noted earlier that both drug trips and masked experiences end. It's an important fact. Someone who intends permanent change and wants something more than a single experience from a day's commitment must realize that real change is a long game. It is in that long game that meditation demonstrates its profundity and enduring value. Having said that, the transitory nature of mask experiences and the liberation from the self they provide are extremely valuable and offer immediate practical applications beyond what I had ever expected of them.

An example: My friend Samantha Paris runs a highly regar voice-acting school in Sausalito, California, named Voicetrax. Sh successful professional voice artist (full disclosure, we met thro common agent) who has thought deeply about her craft and he same way that I work, emphasizing authenticity and which in her parlance she refers to as "finding the bunny." A majority of her students win professional voice-acting work in commercials, cartoons, video games, documentaries, and industrial films.

Several times a year, I run a master class for her senior students, helping them with acting, voice-over work, and general creativity. On the day in question, I had, for the first time, included masks in the first half of an all-day class. The morning was to be dedicated to acting exercise games and masks to promote spontaneity and fearlessness about acting without thought, and the afternoon would be dedicated to listening to them in the recording studio and determining how I could be of use.

At the time, I had no idea why I'd included masks in the day's work, but I must have unconsciously suspected that they could prove useful. The morning's work was fun, and everyone succeeded in finding two or three characters, and as we settled into the grand lunch prepared by Samantha's Italian chef husband, I was pleased by the excitement buzzing through the lunchtime conversations.

After lunch, the plan was that students would read their scripts in the studio sound booth. I always ask that they not see their scripts in advance. I wanted a cold reading to observe them at their most raw and also because that's the way I work, trusting that the first reading of a text produces the most vivid mental associations and automatically adjusts one's emotions (and consequently the voice) to those images. The day's format would be that each student would read while the class listened to his or her performance and my suggestions. Then the student would reread the text with my suggestions in mind, and the class would evaluate the performance.

The first two or three people were advanced students, but they had not finished their training, and neither Sam nor I were satisfied with their efforts. They appeared overly concerned with being good and professional, and this inhibited them. Perhaps they were self-conscious being evaluated by a well-known professional in their field. They well trained, and very polished, but none were particularly unique. All were hampered by professional mannerisms they'd imitated from other narrators, and the early part of the day made me feel as if I were trapped in my car with a radio I could not turn off.

Imitation is a natural impulse. If you listen to very early Ray Charles records, he imitates Nat King Cole and blues singer Charles Brown. Think of the legions of whiny young singers trying to capture Bob Dylan's gritty performances, while Dylan himself evolved into his authentic voice by imitating Woody Guthrie and Ramblin' Jack Elliot. We have all done similar things under the influence of our admiration for another artist because the desire to improve and the pressure to succeed can trick us into forgetting the pithy advice of Oscar Wilde: "Be yourself; everyone else is already taken." I knew that both Samantha and the students themselves expected better work.

Worried that it was going to be a long day, I was not sure how I could help, but on a whim, I asked the young woman in the booth, who was floundering to read her copy again, only this time as one of the characters she had discovered with a mask.

The change was electrifying. The entire class (including Samantha and I) snapped to attention. The reader's voice and psyche were entirely integrated and engaged. The recital became musical, lively, and unpredictable. The students glanced at one another in surprise. The woman's mask performance was radically different from her normal one. The first was professional enough, fluid, and relatively flawless—what my beloved college English professor, Sheldon Zitner, once described as "well rounded and half an inch in diameter." The second was unique, magnetic, and charismatic and *compelled* attention.

The hitch was that the vivid mask character's voice was not appropriate to the text. (Imagine Tony Soprano reading copy for a Rolls-Royce commercial.) I asked her to reread it in her own voice, and this precipitated the second revelation of the day. Her natural voice retained all the discoveries of pace, engagement, storytelling, and music she had discovered with the mask's persona.

It appeared as if her normal psyche had stopped comparing itself to an imagined superior model and had simply "settled in" to itself. In that state, the actress was no longer afraid of submitting to her natural impulses and had ceased censoring out the surprises of colors, emotional tones, and musical variations. She had managed to get out of her own way.

This experiment was successfully repeated thirty times that day, twice for each student, with equal success.

Reviewing the work during a long drive home, I remained elated. Years of mask practice had given me an unshakeable confidence in the positive changes masks can elicit, but I had never witnessed their *utility* before when applied to concrete problem solving. Normally, I taught these mask workshops to Zen students already deeply engaged with issues of consciousness and transformation. As a rule, they were pretty fearless about pushing themselves beyond their comfort zones and skillful at perceiving connections between masked and meditation states. However, this was the first time I had ever used masks with a "civilian" class training for a specific type of work. The positive transference of skills and insights from the masked to the habitual persona was and remains exciting to this day. That discovery became the germinating experience of this book

A PARABLE

When breakfast was over, Buddha gathered the bowls and utensils to wash them. Ever the considerate host, he inquired, "What brings you travelers so far?"

"I'm not at liberty to say," the Lone Ranger replied, ponderously, "but it involves saving mankind."

The Buddha tried to lighten the atmosphere with a joke, saying, "It didn't work out so well for your last guy, did it?" But the Lone Ranger just regarded him blankly and then rose and excused himself.

Double-checking to see that he was unobserved, the Lone Ranger checked his saddlebags again and was relieved to see his stash of silver bullets still undisturbed, the little twigs he'd inserted between them hadn't moved. He lifted the leather flaps attached to the stirrups and was relieved to see his small sack of gold coins still in place, stitched to the leather.

Thinking things through, he decided that, since he could not find Buddy-Boy's hiding place for the food, he didn't have much to fear until it got close to leaving time. He decided the bullets were safe where they were for the time being but did check to ensure that both his pistols were fully loaded. Returning them to their holsters with a tricky double backspin, he straightened up. He was pleased to notice a little less slack in his shirt and slacks from before. The closer he moved toward his old "tailored" self, the better he felt. "We'll hang here a few more days and rebuild ourselves," he decided, and then headed back toward the campfire.

Turning to Tonto, Buddha asked, "Is he serious?"

"Always." Tonto said. "You've given me my first chuckle in ten years."

"But you must have a job to do, no?

"The truth is we're a couple of has-beens. Clayton used to be a huge star, and I trailed in his wake. My best guess is they dropped the show, and the writers left in midscript, leaving us high and dry. Most people have these crazy ideas about actors, but somebody else writes the stories. We can't speak if they don't put words in our mouths. Anyway, somehow we got out here, but we've got no idea what happens next."

"Just like real life," Buddha responded pleasantly and then added in an offhand way, "But you don't need a script to 'act' yourself, do you?"

Tonto liked Buddha's easy manner with him. No bullshit. "No," he admitted, "but times change, and we're trying to hold on to what we had, I guess."

"That's a recipe for suffering," the Buddha responded. "If you try to stop the tides, you'll drown."

Tonto regarded him steadily. "I know who you are, you know. I've read about you and a little bit about your teachings. But you don't look like a god to me."

"I'm not. I'm just a human being. A lucky human. Born into a healthy body and free to study wisdom."

"So, what're you doin' here, then?"

"I came because the world needed me," the Buddha responded simply.

Tonto laughed. "You sound like Clayton," he said.

The Buddha laughed with him. "I suppose," he said, "except I don't shoot people." They both cracked up.

"The guy needs help. He has no idea what to eat or how to find water. He's lost in thought most of the time, but he's a good guy. He fought for me in Hollywood," Tonto offered.

"I get it," Buddha replied. "You're a bodhisattva."

"No, actually I'm a Mohawk, for whatever that's worth," Tonto answered.

"You can be both. A bodhisattva is someone whose life is dedicated to helping others."

"Well, this was our gig, and we had good times. I'm not gonna be the first to bail on him," Tonto answered.

"But you need help, too, don't you," Buddha said, and it wasn't a question.

Tonto thought about it a moment. "Yes," he said slowly. "Yes, I guess I do."

At this juncture, Tonto is a man who has seen or heard of the Buddha and may have some idea or instinct about him. His vision is not as occluded with personal agendas as the Lone Ranger's is, and he is candid enough to admit that he's in some trouble—the first step toward any positive change.

6

Inviting the Shock of Recognition

The moment that lives most vividly for me was that millisecond when I looked in the mirror and saw my "self" in the mask for the first time. Right then I was a blank slate. What a gift. I can't recall ever experiencing that before. Then, with a few movements, someone completely new and different emerged, and she let me know exactly who she was. A thrill of discovery coupled with the relief of shedding the everyday expectation of who I think I am! Beautiful.

LIZ, WORKSHOP PARTICIPANT

Because our ideas of the self are usually intuitive and immediate, it's necessary to clarify some of these ideas before trying on a mask. If not, the mind-body resistance will stifle impulses as they arise, attempting to defend the self. What follows is a series of exercises, most drawn from the training of actors. Some may appear silly, generate anxiety, or appear unrelated to any spiritual intention, but they have specific purposes. Be patient with them. They are important to deflect self-consciousness and habitual ego defenses by moving the body and mind through unusual, sometimes awkward or unsettling, experiences in a nonthreatening environment. Ignoring them often muffles the clarity of recognition when you place a mask over your face and see it in a mirror.

In an interesting book titled *The Golden Buddha Changing Masks: An Opening to Transformative Theatre,* the author Mark Olsen, an actor and member of the renowned Mummenschanz Swiss mask theater troupe, examines the connections and reciprocity between acting and spiritual pursuits. He cites Richard Schechner's answer to the question: What do actors *do*? Schechner, a performance theorist from NYU's Tisch School of the Arts, responded with *restored behavior,* a term he coined, which he explained as follows:

> Restored behavior is . . . *a depiction of the self, usually perceived as stationary and fixed, as really being a role or set of roles.* In short, actors give evidence of the ephemeral aspect of the personality, while reaffirming essential human unity. [author's italics][1]

Our unquestioned habits of posture, thought, behavior, and intentions resist being exposed; they are ephemeral, like bats hiding from daylight. They feel like *us* and appear to possess physical permanence. These games and exercises offer the body cumulative, nonverbal confidence that rendering the ego temporarily inoperable is *safe*. If "no one's home" who will fear leaping into the unknown? Furthermore, these games introduce body and mind to the "something else" (what Buddhists refer to as Big Mind), which has always existed as a substrate immensely larger than our personal ideas and beliefs. This "something else" responds to our intentions for growth and positive change if we allow it to.

The most practical mechanisms I've discovered for enhancing confidence in Big Mind—aside from meditation—are games like these that urge us to act without deliberation or a safety net, fearless as to what we might reveal. They are particularly useful for uncovering *the edges of the self*—for catching glimpses and clarifying our ideas of who we really are. Just try them, even at home, and see what you learn.

I refer to many of these exercises as games because they have rules and forms, like football, baseball, or basketball. Rules and forms create limitations, which not only add difficulty but also offer us common metrics against which we measure our skill. Without structure, games would be chaotic. These games are akin to the forms in Zen practice, which offer us an extrapersonal way of sitting, standing, and meditating that we can use as a standard to see how well we're paying attention.

The attentiveness and skills required to play these games and thus be nurtured by them can be extended to every waking moment. This practice is sometimes referred to as mindfulness.

Like intelligence, mindfulness per se has no inherent moral valence, and employing it to make a business more profitable, win negotiations, dominate discourse, and perform questionable work more efficiently ignores the root compassion of Buddha's teaching and his fundamental intention of saving all beings. Mindfulness becomes a function of spiritual practice only when intention is firmly fixed on ensuring that all intentions and actions are *always* based on kindness, helpfulness, and compassion.

For Buddhists, mindfulness is grounded in the realization that everything—substantial and insubstantial—is interdependent, that each apparently separate thing is inextricably related to and made of other things. Consequently, the idea of an absolutely independent self, which stands isolated from the rest of creation, is an illusion. For Buddhists, mindfulness is always rooted in this deep sense of *interbeing,* which is Vietnamese Zen master Thich Nhat Hanh's lovely term for dependent origination. Excising mindfulness from its ethical matrix is like clearcutting the Amazon to produce palm oil to prevent sunburn. That is not mindfulness; it is myopia.

Although these games usually occur in the context of a class, many of them can be done alone and at home with beneficial results. However, the first three Circle Song games require a group.

Ⓢ CIRCLE SONG 1

This is one of my favorite games and perhaps the simplest—making up a group story song, with each person contributing one line. It is dirt simple—until we add the relentless pressure of time.

The class sits in a circle. The teacher establishes a rhythm by clapping or using a drum. The class mimics the rhythm and is instructed *to maintain it without wavering*. Once the beat is established, the teacher offers the first line of a sing-song story, any four-beat line will do (capitalized letters represent stresses synchronized with the rhythm): "I WENT downTOWN to STEAL a CAR." Skip one beat, and on the *next,* the entire class chants, "DO RUN-RUN-RUN, DO RUN-RUN."

The next contributor must begin her line on the *very next beat* following the last "RUN," and that person is charged with advancing the story line. For instance: "I SAW a little HONDA with the KEYS inSIDE," or "it HAD to be YELLOW, could NOT be BLUE." If a person is unable to think of anything to say, he or she must still maintain the rhythm and meter and fill his allotted space with nonsense sounds, like "buh-BLAH, buh-BLAH, buh-BLAH, buh-BLAH," for the length of time they would have spoken. Skip one beat, and the class chants, "DO RUN-RUN-RUN," and so on. *On the next beat,* the next person picks up the thread. This is the simplest form of the game, but it is never so simple that people won't balk, freeze, or collapse with anxiety. The anxiety of not knowing what line you will receive makes it impossible to plan ahead, and leaping in without knowing what you'll do raises all sorts of nonharmful anxiety, which is one point of the exercise.

By the second or third round, nearly everyone is able to chime in, in rhythm, more relaxed and in good humor, and able to advance a coherent (if ridiculous) story line. The first time the class achieves 100 percent participation, the students always break into spontaneous applause. Then, the teacher raises the stakes by dropping the DO-RUN-RUN (time to think), which means that as soon as one person finishes, the next person has only one beat before she must begin. Most people hesitate and lose the rhythm or become paralyzed by being forced to act without preparation. Their discomfort is a source of much glee for their classmates. When people are unable to improvise, it's usually because they are self-conscious, are too intent on wanting to be good, or are protecting themselves from revealing unconscious mental freight. When people try this exercise at home, they probably will not suffer from self-consciousness, but during class, we take a break and offer an antidote I learned from Keith Johnstone, which he calls the Bad Singing Game.

⟨Ṣ⟩ THE BAD SINGING GAME

Participants are instructed to render a chosen song in the worst possible way they can. No matter how off-key, tonelessly, or badly they sing, the teacher urges them to "be worse." There's a little voice inside most of us that wants us to be perfect or the best, or it wants to protect us from embarrassment and resists this instruction, and that impulse of self-protection can sabotage our internal freedom. This game attacks that instinct head-on.

By the end of the Bad Singing Game, self-consciousness will, for the most part, have been banished from the room. (The teacher always supports players who mess up by assuming responsibility for their failures: "Sorry, I'm a terrible teacher. I didn't teach you well enough.") It is important to lower the stakes for failure as the difficulties of the exercises increase.

Another way to break up self-consciousness and to presage what will occur later when masks are introduced is to charge each person with imitating one of his parents and addressing the class as that parent. There is no one who cannot mimic one of her parents.

⟨Ṣ⟩ CIRCLE SONG 2

In the next iteration, players are asked to rhyme lines in an A-A B-B pattern—that is, the second person ends their line rhyming with the last word of the person before them. The third person establishes a new rhyme, which the fourth person must rhyme. Every addition of a new wrinkle usually leads to faltering and "blah-blah-ing." However, players will be more experienced by now and more fearless about their efforts.

᯼ CIRCLE SONG 3

The third version of the Circle Song creates an A-B-A-B rhyme pattern. The third participant rhymes the first person's last word, and the fourth rhymes the second person's last word. Once students begin to trust the mind's ability to supply what's needed, fear diminishes, and it's surprising how readily and with what invention adults will play (and enjoy) a game like this. The skills developed in these games promote fearlessness, confidence, poise, and relaxation in the face of uncertainty and pressure. Most important, they facilitate trust in the boundless well of Big Mind—the processes and understanding beyond control of our conscious mind. These games become precursors for spontaneous responses and improvisation in unexpected situations in any area of life.

These chanting games might account for a half hour of class time, and when folks have loosened up, it's time to begin behavior exercises. These games, as well, are simple but build skills and cumulatively impart useful information.

We all have rote behaviors we rely on in social situations, and we rarely question or seek alternatives to them. Theoretically, human behavior is infinitely variable, but when it's filtered through fixed ideas and attitudes about a permanent self, choices are constricted, and we make instantaneous decisions about what is and is not "us." Behavior games push people beyond their comfort zones and allow the body to *experience* sensations and emotional information normally filtered out of awareness.

᯼ POSTURE IS YOUR IDEA OF WHO YOU ARE

Try to imagine where in your body you conceive yourself to reside. The head? Chest? Stomach? Behind the eyes? Resting on the back teeth? Amble around with that question and try to determine from what place your body appears to initiate movement. Maintain your awareness on that spot while you determine if this is how you normally move. Does examining this question cause you to behave differently?

The game that follows is a way to deepen that exploration. It's simple, but it will trigger surprising feelings and shake the body out of its routines. It may feel too silly to be important, but once again, we are addressing the body and not our intellect, so even an act, which appears meaningless, can offer the body safe experiences of behaving in a "not-self" manner.

⎙ THE RED DOT GAME

Imagine a small red dot, like a laser, that is under your control. You can place it anywhere on the body you like, and it will designate the spot from where your movements will be initiated.

Begin by placing the laser dot on the spot where you imagine normal is and begin walking around. Does it feel right? If not, experiment by moving it to another place until you find your normal.

Once normal has been established, in class I ask everyone to place the dot on the tip of their nose and let it pull them through space as if the tip of the nose were dragging the rest of the body along. Try it at home. *Exaggerate* at first. Let your nose stick out well in advance of your body. How does it feel? Nosy? Pushy? Inquisitive? Like a dog following a scent? Like the cartoon Ichabod Crane? Play with those feelings and track the images that arise in mind as your physical adjustments change. You may not always remain in the human realm—no worries. Just try to be faithful to the images you imagine.

Catalogue how these images make you feel. Then, by degrees, dial back your exaggeration until you could walk about in the street and no one would consider you odd. Make a note to "take it outside" and practice being in and among people with this new posture, and stay alert to discover any new responses generated in yourself and, importantly, in others by this posture.

Now put the dot on your chin and walk with your chin leading. Are you comfortable or uncomfortable with this adjustment? Do you feel pushy, aggressive, stubborn, proud? How is it different from the habitual you? Move around and interact with classmates (or the public) and remain attentive to how it changes your feelings. Once that has been established, begin to dial back the exaggeration, settling a few moments at each new position to see how it affects your feeling and self-image. Continue dialing it back until it could pass for normal on the street. "Passing for normal" does not mean abandoning that site and the information it provides you. The trick is to keep your attention focused on that spot to learn how it affects you. Does it bolster your confidence, or does it feel too aggressive? Does it remind you of someone? If so, what happens to your feelings if you invoke that person clearly, wearing *him* as a mask in your imagination and acting it out subtly enough to take it outside?

Place the red dot on your chest. (Often, women with prominent breasts will tuck their posture by rolling their shoulders forward to deemphasize them.) Try to remove any sexual connotations from this posture and experience it as *expansion*—claiming your space. Or, if as a woman you find yourself paying too much attention to your breasts, concentrate on the rigidity of the sternum itself.

Try to stay with whatever images and feelings arise. Explore your discomforts, and don't let yourself escape from these new feelings too impulsively and without exploring them. Class (or your own home) is a safe space to experiment. With your chest out, do you feel more powerful? Armored? As if you're showing off? Is it too aggressive? Sexual? Does it generate associations of other people, and if so, who? There is no right answer to these questions, but whatever you feel is valuable information about the way you have defined yourself and your associations. File them, because summoning them will regenerate these feelings, and particularly for performers of any kind, they will add more crayons to your box of available responses.

What happens if you accept these feelings and become one of those people in your mind's eye? When you've identified your feelings and can accept or face them without flinching, dial back the posture so you could pass undetected on the street and see how it affects your self-image outside class (or your home).

Continue experimenting with different positions of the red dot.

Place the red dot on your stomach.
Place the red dot on your groin.
Place it on one shoulder and then the other.
Place it on one knee or the other.

Make a quick note of how each adjustment alters your sense of self and generates unfamiliar impulses and sensations. In each case pay attention to the oddness or rightness of how you feel and determine in as precise a manner as you can what and why a posture makes you comfortable or uncomfortable. What feels right is your habitual self. What feels odd could be the basis of something fresh and surprising that is seeking expression.

Try not to be concerned with what others might think of you; focus on how *you* feel. If you find yourself becoming concerned with the opinions of others, realize that their imagined thoughts are actually *yours*. You have no idea what they're thinking. Catalogue those thoughts and note the way you adjust to them. This comfort-discomfort zone is the inline and outline of your sense of self. Is it a habitual for you to reside here? If I were to ask you who the model for your internal critic is, could you tell me? Does your daily behavior generally play to an audience or a specific person in your mind's eye? Are you more concerned with what *she* might think or feel, or your own feelings? If it's her opinion, ask yourself why you might elevate the opinions of people over your own. Such questions are portals through which one catches glimpses of the self's normally invisible edges.

Whatever you feel is okay, and no one can criticize your feelings, but *whatever you are liking and disliking are direct expressions of whom you believe you are.* Big Mind, like the sky, receives everything without judgment. The sun shines on the people you like and don't. Try to determine whether these likes and dislikes *originated* with you or are *received* values that you somehow absorbed. Whatever you feel, it's important to remember that once you identify and name a moment or memory that identification becomes a snapshot—frozen in time, no longer a fully living, constantly mutating awareness.

Try taking these red dot practices out on the street (best if you're in a spot where people don't know you), even if briefly, perhaps as you pass through a checkout line in a market. Use such opportunities to catalogue responses that differ from those you'd normally anticipate. Do they correspond with what you imagined or with how you might respond to such a person? If your altered behavior changes the responses of others positively, tag it for memory and adopt it. Why not? What is there inside you besides habits and ideas of who you are to prevent you? If they're habits that don't serve you, drop them; if they're ideas, review them to see if they're sound and still worth being loyal to. Where did you get them and on what are they based? See if you can identify the first time you concluded that they were a fixed feature of your internal geography.

By the same token, if a reaction startles or disturbs you, you can always practice what Buddhists call one-breath practice. Exhale gently and focus your attention strictly on that exhale, feeling the air pass the edges of your nostrils, sending it out into the world as if it were a child you were wishing well. By the end of that exhale, your mind will have cleared. No one will know that you're doing it, but it will fix you firmly into the present moment. I repeat this practice before answering the phone, or when I'm asked to make an important decision or to meet or counsel people. It helps me meet the current moment without expectations or habitual responses. Try it and see what you think.

We needn't fear the force and allure of our minds once we have confidence that we can observe them from a detached perch, immune to being snatched away by our compelling internal narratives. Concentrating on our breath and posture anneals us to the present moment, and stillness (in meditation, for instance) denies the mind stimulus, allowing it to calm *itself* naturally. From this perch, regarding our mental movies with detachment, we can allow our thoughts to be our thoughts without fear of our awareness being borne away to places we can't abide. The bounty for this practice is freedom. The liberated imagination is playful and begins to affect us positively, bestowing a stream of imagery and power that professional artists of every discipline have learned to ride in the same way that surfers ride a wave—simultaneously in and out of control.

The idea that there is an organ corresponding to a "captain" within us "steering our ship," doing our seeing, hearing, thinking, and so forth, is both cumbersome and inaccurate. Can you imagine the impossible speed required for such a captain to direct a great basketball player while he is playing—shouting out commands for moves, feints, sleights, and so forth? An athlete's responses are occurring at the speed of awareness. There is no time to receive communiqués from the wheelhouse. Learning to release the idea of a captain or some other surrogate for the self from its wheelhouse is an important technique for getting out of our own way, short-circuiting doublethinking, back talk, and self-doubt to achieve the expansive awareness and dialed-in focus necessary for peak performance.

In the captain's cabin (our imagined locus of self), the walls are decorated with snapshots of our lives at different ages and times: family members, school chums, childhood homes, all the mosaic pieces constituting the objective evidence certifying who we are. Among these are Post-it Notes with simple descriptions of who we believe we are, composed of things we have been told or implied about ourselves from circumstances. The accumulation of these photos and Post-it Notes becomes the armature of what we automatically refer to as our self.

Our faith in this evidence overlooks the fact that each photo and each Post-it Note is a frozen entity. A photograph is 125th of a second. In a moment of pique, your mother or father utters harsh words to you. Ten minutes later, they may forget what they said, but if their words affected you sufficiently, they may remain on your wheelhouse wall forever. All such frozen moments bear the same relationship to self-awareness a mummy bears to a living being.

The captain can leave the cabin from time to time without endangering the ship, and so can we. Things will continue to run on autopilot. Such vacations from the strictures of rigid identity are what meditation, psychedelics, masks, and total immersion in what occupies us supply—moments to surrender control to Big Mind, to allow ourselves to be surprised by who we are. Such breaks are critical to good health, confidence, and relaxation. You may not trust yourself, but you were generated by what produced hummingbirds and wolves, sunrise and the patter of rain. There's no need to worry about becoming permanently lost because our habitual self is our default position. We will return to it—but return with the knowledge that it is a temporary dwelling and not a jail.

When we are young and without agency to challenge the omnipotent giants raising us, it's normal to absorb their judgments and declarations as gospel truth. We have not yet understood that those adults were once threatened, befuddled, and confused in the same ways we are, locked in their own captains' cabins, their walls also adorned with their own photos and declarative Post-it Notes.

Reexamining such feelings and bringing mature experience to bear on them, even debating them (aloud) with our own unconscious, is another liberating practice that inoculates us against such invisible parasites. We can't hold on to a good mood, so why worry about a bad mood? They're both shadows, clouds temporarily shading our internal luminosity. As we have learned to live with seasonal and daily changes of weather, we can learn to live with the vagaries of our own internal climate, and meditation is the practice by which we discover the detachment required to do so.

Detachment is a prerequisite for the sustained commitment required for the mind-body to relax, to release buried information from storage to consciousness. This requires dedicating the same effort to understanding our minds and personal biases and habits we have dedicated to memorizing batting averages or free-throw statistics, the names of fashion houses and clothing designers, or pertinent data on various automobiles. Unlike such catalogues, efforts at self-discovery pay off in permanent positive change.

The purpose of these exercises (with and without masks) is to formalize investigation and offer guidelines and markers as aids to ourselves in the same way that mountain climbers drive pitons into a rock face to secure safety line holds. Becoming aware of how feelings rise from nowhere, assemble in our awareness, and crystallize as judgment, pride, doubt, vanity, or shame and how, if we attach to them, they can drag us around for a lifetime will stimulate our practice of releasing them. Rising and falling like breath, like our individuated lives, they assume temporary coherence and then pass away. What is there to fear?

A PARABLE

One morning, a few days later, Tonto and the Lone Ranger awoke to discover Buddha sitting in deep meditation. He was as impervious to their queries as if he were surrounded by an invisible force field. The Lone Ranger was miffed and kept demanding breakfast. Tonto was fascinated.

Around lunchtime, Buddha rose and announced that he needed to speak to them. Uncovering a bowl of cooked seeds and grains sweetened with honey (and whispering to the ants in the bowl that they had eaten enough and now must leave—which they did), he made sure the Lone Ranger and Tonto had food and plenty of sage tea before he began speaking. He appeared shaky and weak to them, suddenly sallow.

"I know you have important work to do," he began, speaking to the

Lone Ranger directly. "And I know how important it is that you fight evil. I was wondering if it's as important for you to do good?"

"Absolutely," the Lone Ranger responded, suddenly interested in this curious fellow and his drift. "Why?"

"Because I need help," Buddha responded. "I'm in trouble. I'm dying, and I'm afraid I could leave this world before my master returns, and his goods could be scattered or stolen by thieves."

"Good Lord!" the Lone Ranger exclaimed, feigning concern, but to himself thinking, "Maybe I misjudged this guy."

Tonto said nothing but felt something wasn't right. He observed the Buddha carefully.

"Yes," Buddha replied. "This is the spot where I'm to die, but if you would stay and help me build a secure structure, it could be both my tomb and the repository for my master's treasure. I would see that you and the horses stay fed and healthy and inform my master of your efforts on his behalf. I am confident that he would want to reward you with gifts of immense value."

"Now, we're gettin' somewhere," the Lone Ranger thought.

Tonto thought, "This is bullshit . . . but it's good bullshit."

That night, after the Buddha had retired, Tonto and the Lone Ranger sat up whispering.

"Our luck has changed, Tonto. This man must have some serious loot hidden away. We could build him his little house, win the gratitude of his master, and get a grubstake that would set us up back in Hollywood. Jesus, maybe we'd have enough to back a new film." The Lone Ranger laughed out loud. "Back to the good old days."

"I'm not sure, guy," Tonto replied. "This fellow is up to something. He's actually famous, did you know that? His name is Buddha, and people all over the world regard him as a god. He's no servant. He doesn't feel bent to me, but his story is not straight up either."

The Lone Ranger was undeterred. "Hey," he responded, "they used to regard me as a god, remember? We've both wound up in the same *place. Things happen for a reason. Only we're lost, and he's not. We're broke, and he isn't."*

"Whatever," Tonto replied, "but I'm with you."

The Sanskrit word *upaya* is a term in Buddhist practice signifying "skillful means." It refers to the fact that even enlightenment is of no use to others if we don't apply our discernment to understanding *how* to communicate so that the individual with whom we're speaking can understand.

The Buddha is not sick, merely employing his understanding of the Lone Ranger to snare him for a compassionate purpose.

7
You Think It's a Game? Try It!

When Peter Coyote asked me to wear a mask, I found that rather than being hidden [by it], I was emboldened. This was not what I expected after just finishing an emotional exercise where I had been asked to impersonate a parent, both of whom I had lost in recent years.

A tilt of the head per Peter's instructions, and I was Brandi, a very sexual, confident character. At one point I snapped back to [my normal] reality and exclaimed, "Oh my goodness, I am hitting on Peter Coyote," but he raised the mirror, and I was immediately Brandi again. How simple and yet how powerful. What surprised me even further was how my Brandi character helped me with a narration later in the day. Performing as someone else released me from "me" and all my insecurities. And yes, after class I bought myself a mask.

LYNN DOUGLAS, A.K.A. BRANDI,
VOICETRAX STUDENT

INTENTION

Every actor (and every Buddhist) is familiar with the term *intention*. For Buddhists, intention represents the only thing in the universe that we can control. Because our monkey mind is so active, available to impulse and sensation and quixotic, the Buddhist practice of mindfulness is dedicated to remaining in the present moment (avoiding distractions of impulses and desires) and focusing intention on compassion—fixing it there with the force of habit. When this is well established, we can be fairly certain that even unpremeditated responses to situations will be helpful or kind.

For actors, intention is what your character *wants or needs to accomplish* in a given scene or in their arc of the play. The *strategy* the character employs to achieve this will determine how that character behaves. For instance, two men might enter a public restroom to relieve themselves. One leaves, wiping his hands on his pants; the other washes and dries his hands and uses the paper towel to turn the doorknob. Judgment aside, their behavior reveals very different mental states.

In a dramatic scene, one might need to discover if a partner has been faithful or find the combination to a safe. The script might require an actor to browbeat, dismiss, or encourage someone. Some will achieve this by guile, some by threat, some by encouragement. The *way* in which a character fulfills his or her task reveals who that character is. Virtually any verb can express an intention, but when introducing the subject to nonactors, it's helpful to take a moment to discuss the distinction between *acting* and *pretending*.

Acting is human behavior. We realize a person is happy when he or she *acts* happy, and we understand when someone is angry by their behavior as well. *Pretending* involves copying the superficial externals of behavior without supporting the behavior internally with specific imagery that actually generates the emotion. There are people who are very skilled in mimicking behavior and its emotional components— among them actors, salesmen, con men, and politicians. Human beings have evolved sensitive receptors for distinguishing between real and simulated behavior. Deciding whether we believe someone—whether a salesman, a doctor, a financial adviser, a lover, or a real-estate agent—is serious business because mistaking faked behavior for true can have long-term deleterious consequences.

Actors (swindlers, politicians, and con men) cannot afford to be caught pretending. The problem for actors arises when they are called upon to do something they might not believe in or agree with, may never have done, or are morally repulsed by. In most cases, they will choose an ordinary behavior that when honestly executed will read appropriately for the situation. One of the actors in the film *The French Connection* decided to play his death by gunfire as if he had just leaped into a freezing shower. I've never murdered anyone, but in a film once, I shot a man as if I were swatting a fly—something I'd done many times—which made me appear to be a heartless killer.

Many actors are challenged by less-than-excellent scripts, and one method we employ to circumvent such dilemmas without lying is by employing the fig leaf of *as-if*. As-if is like a magical suture stitching a player's imagination to the task at hand. I've never tortured anyone, but if I were called upon to do so in a role and performed the task as if I were testing and analyzing the repair of my car's motor or trying to choose which mouse I would feed to a pet snake, I would appear chillingly vicious. If I chose to torture him as if I were playing a party game with children, all three of which I have done, I'd appear to be a psychopath.

Humans are skilled at detecting lying and pretense and generally very good at identifying authentic behavior. All skilled actors have learned that the more *specifically* they imagine a particular event, the more vigorously it will excite their imagination and generate authentic behavior. When that happens, their emotions will be universally understood. It defies logic, but it is 100 percent true that a performer's *specificity* of imagery is most viscerally appreciable to an audience. I believe the reason is that while our personal histories are unique, the underlying emotions are universal. When a person's imagination ignites true emotions (always generated by specific details), those emotions are perceived empathically by observers. This empathy is the basis of all performing arts. What follows are some further exercises that sensitize the nervous system to impulse and intuition—critical for accepting the inputs of a mask when one meets it.

⟲ AS-IF PRACTICE

The entire class is assembled on one side of the room. The teacher explains the simple action required of each participant. Upon hearing a knock, the actors are to walk to the door and open it. Before the first actor begins, the teacher offers her an as-if instruction: "Walk to the door *as if* you don't want to wake the baby." Other possibilities are as if "it's the cute guy you met at Starbucks and faked into helping you with your computer," "the boyfriend you just broke up with," or "your son who's been out all night." Each actor is given a simple narrative on which to base his or her behavior.

The teacher knocks, and the first player expresses the assignment as best they can. After each performance, the teacher queries the students to evaluate the behavior for veracity and detail. Did the behavior seem appropriate to the task? Did class members believe it? If not, why not? What were the tells that made the students doubt the performer? Had they seen such behavior before, or did this evocation appear fresh and original?

After the criticism has been heard, the actor is asked to repeat the action, but this time the teacher insists that they take a moment to ground *specific* details about the circumstances into their mind. Imagine the room they are in. What does it indicate about the person who lives there? Is it filled with bookshelves and art? Spare and cold? Fashion magazines? Men's magazines? Tools? What are the colors? The actor is challenged to closely imagine the person they are about to represent—the more detail the better. What is it you like about this person? What are you nervous about? What are the complexities of your relationship? Are you embarrassed about the cleanliness of your room, for instance? Have you left the filthy plate out that your son pushed away when he left the table? These are the sorts of questions actors answer as they become intimate with the text during rehearsals. This is the work of an actor.

The actors in class are urged to pay attention to their imaginations and intuitive responses and not try to observe themselves objectively from without. When they do that, the change in their authenticity and the belief this change generates in audiences is remarkable, and those changes are reflected in the class notes afterward.

The purpose of my classes is *not* to train actors but to encourage people to tune in to and commit to the imagination, including the images, snatches of dialogue, and impulses that arrive over the spinal telephone—all the snatch-and-grab moments that communicate our inner life to us. They are rehearsals of fidelity to their inner life, a critical step in sensitizing people to what will occur later when they don a mask. On another level, more relevant to Buddhist study and practice, it is also an important antecedent to self-acceptance and a satisfying life. We can consider these clearly imagined mental images as masks themselves, blocking self-consciousness and distraction, leaving the actor free to respond to inner directives.

🗒 WHISPERED INTENTION

After everyone has had a turn, we begin again, only this time the teacher *whispers* the intention to the actor, often with a mini-narrative for context.

> You've been having a really tough time with your sixteen-year-old. She has been stealing your liquor, and you're afraid she might be experimenting with drugs. You hear her coming in two hours late, and when she knocks, you know she's forgotten her keys—additional evidence of her irresponsibility.

After the actor has answered the door, in accordance with this narrative, the students (who do not know the intention) are queried to see if they can determine the actor's instructions.

Far more often than not, if the actor has fully inhabited the task, the class can identify very specific details of the narrative and will often guess the entire story quite precisely. Even when they don't, they will describe many specific emotional states deriving from the instructions. This only occurs when the performer's imagination has been activated by very specific and personal images.

SELF-CONSCIOUSNESS AND SHAME

When I was a young boy, I often responded to my parents' hypervigilant concerns and criticism with a sense of insufficiency and depression, saddened because I felt that I constantly displeased them. In fifth and sixth grades, I became preoccupied with a self-comforting practice of imagining an ideal self by inventing a composite personality, grafting admired qualities of my schoolmates onto my own images of myself. On a given day I might have said, "I wish I had Mike Taylor's physique, Dick Vann's shrewd calmness (and family), Tanny Glidden's agility and courage, Tommy Chagaris's style." I desperately wanted a better version of myself as a balm to my wounded self-esteem and to please my parents. Aggregating the best qualities of my friends seemed like the most direct route to that goal. Recalling the persistence of that preoccupation today, I can see now how each of those attributes represented the desire for a mask. No matter how dissatisfied I was, I never considered giving away my own thinking— which I'd failed to recognize as the real source of most of my problems.

🔊 NAKED BEFORE THE MIRROR

Here's an exercise to do at home. Strip naked and stand before a full-length mirror. Review your body carefully and catalogue the feelings about it that arise as you examine yourself. Which parts do you like? Which embarrass you or fail to meet your standards? Take a moment to consider where those standards developed or how they were delivered to you. Are these other people's standards or your own? Now imagine that you are standing with this naked body before an auditorium filled with strangers.

Would you be proud? Ashamed? Embarrassed? Confident? Consider the situation amusing?

Explore your emotional associations to your naked physical self. What are your judgments and satisfactions? In what *physical details* are your embarrassments or pride lodged? More important, can you identify the comparisons or judgments that are eliciting your responses? Most important, what do these judgments reveal about you, the judge?

This is a useful practice for ferreting out the ways we often make automatic, destructive judgments of ourselves based on unconscious comparisons with other individuals or mass-market ideals. Suzuki-roshi once reminded his students, "Everything is perfect until you compare."

In our hyperbolic commercial environment, personal attractiveness has been amplified as a primary status attribute, fueling the music, film, beauty, fashion, and consumer-products industries as well as influencing our personal anxieties and desires. Because we are genetically wired to notice attractive people and physical characteristics that suggest fertility and virility, such attraction may appear to be a hardwired mandate against which we are powerless, but that is not the case. We are also hardwired for aggression and yet, in most cases, train ourselves to restrain such impulses.

We can retrain our instincts if we observe them clearly enough and realize that they are not impressed into a pre-formed identity. They are impulses and projections, but even a brief review of people we might assume have it all reveals lives afflicted with drug abuse, repeated rehabs, suicide attempts, vicious divorce battles, and legal infractions. The tarnished lives of the rich and famous should remind us that beauty is also a mask, and the desires beauty rouses in us *may* be just the cheese in evolution's mousetrap. Beauty and our response to it is another doorway through which to meet the self.

A PARABLE

Over a breakfast of quail eggs, boiled nettles spiced with sage, and some more of the wild desert grains—which were, the Lone Ranger had to admit, delicious when toasted—the Buddha sketched on paper the plan for the structure. The house would have both a tomb and a room to store the treasure—which the Lone Ranger, despite repeated searches, had not been able to find.

The plan was not overly ambitious. One room would be sealed up for the Buddha's tomb and the other sealed with a massive door to guard his master's treasure. His master would arrive "any day," and their reward for their efforts would be immense. When the Lone Ranger tried to broach the subject—subtly of course—the Buddha squeezed a gold coin from the hem of his robe, revealed it for a moment, and then slid it back.

The Lone Ranger was galvanized. "Man," he thought, "this could be serious gelt. Maybe his master might want to bank a film. I'm not too old yet. Tonto's still lookin' good."

The house was simple enough, but the problem, they all agreed, was that it had to be made of stone because nothing else was more durable. If a man wanted a tomb or a bank vault, he ought to build it to last. The Lone Ranger concurred with that idea, even as he tried to recall what had happened to the cemetery plot he and his last wife had once bought.

Over the next month, they gathered rocks—prying loose boulders and rolling them onto a log sled, which Silver obligingly pulled into position. They worked like coolies. The Lone Ranger had to admit that Buddy-Boy was a working fool. He worked from sunup to sundown, without complaint or flagging. He could carry his own body weight in stone, and his precision with a chisel and hammer was extraordinary.

By the end of the third rock-lifting, humping, grunting day, the Lone Ranger was growing suspicious that the cunning little foreigner might be hustling them. He'd been taken before; Hollywood had seen to that. So he asked Buddy-Boy for some reassurance that his master would honor his promise and they would be paid. This time, Buddy-Boy revealed two gold coins and said that if he died before his master returned, the Lone Ranger should take all the coins from the hem of his garment and also the map revealing where his master's treasure was buried. This focused the Lone Ranger's mind to an extraordinary degree, and he threw himself into his labor with renewed vigor.

One evening after several more weeks of hard work, he stripped down to pour a bucket of water over himself and wash away the day's dust and grit. He was startled to notice that his scrawniness had begun to disappear. He could discern traces of his old acrobat's body—the shadow of a six-pack outlining his stomach. The crepe-paper skin around his arms and pecs was now stretched taut by the reemergence of muscle.

Swelling with pride, he wrapped a towel around himself and revisited his train of thought about how the Buddha came up with all the unlikely tools they needed to continue. So far, he'd found no hint of his stash. He walked over to the fire and noticed Tonto sitting in his loincloth, already washed. He looked fifteen years younger—bronzed, lean as a weasel, and strong. The Lone Ranger smiled to himself and thought, "We're back!"

The Lone Ranger continues to pick and choose—good and bad, discriminating what he likes from what he doesn't. His monkey mind is still active, sublimating everything around himself to his plan to "get back to Hollywood." The work is changing his body and in some ways placing him more firmly within it; he is noticing details like Buddha's strength and endurance and remembering his own previous physicality.

8
The Imaginary Performance

My experience with the masks was just as amazing as last year—perhaps more so, since this time I trusted that a character would appear [when I wore the mask]. The prompting to tilt my head, widen my eyes, etc., while looking into the mirror was very helpful, and the characters rose up from within me almost immediately! As Peter asked questions . . . the answers simply appeared, with hardly a thought and very little anxiety. (I've purchased a few masks online and am looking forward to experimenting with them at home!)

NINA GREELEY, VOICETRAX STUDENT

We all spend some portion of our time lost in imaginary worlds, talking to ourselves, entertaining alluring fantasies, exacting imagined revenge, reiterating old arguments, or reenacting what the French refer to as *l'esprit d'escalier*—the spirit of the stairs—realizing on the way out the perfect rejoinder to someone at the party you just left. We often do this without being fully aware of it, until we surprise ourselves by speaking aloud on the street.

One of the important dynamics we retain in memory is being observed lovingly or critically by a person who is or was very important to us, usually a parent, a favorite teacher, an aunt, or an uncle. Depending on the observer's gaze, we can feel buoyant and confident or unsure and intimidated. This is another corridor on which to encounter the self.

The next time you walk down the street, study the people you pass and see if you receive any intuition that one of them might be performing for someone in *their own* mind's eye. Do you feel any projection coming from them—physical assertion, sublimated threat, worry, concern, amusement, and flirtation? Study the faces as if they were masks and try to identify their dominant quality or attitude.

If you receive a clear impression, imagine whether that quality might be the projection of an identity they favor or perhaps an alteration to disguise something they're uncomfortable with. Are they behaving in a manner that might please an important someone from their past or behaving as if they might be trying to protect themself from negative judgments? Try to justify your hunch with specific evidence: Are they relaxed or tense? Apparently enjoying themself or not? Do they seem present or preoccupied in mental realms?

⟨§⟩ THE LOVING-CRITICAL WITNESS

Pick a person who you feel loves and supports you and always extends you the benefit of the doubt. Set a timer for fifteen minutes. Keeping that person in the forefront of your mind, go about your daily routine— washing the dishes, helping kids with homework, speaking on the phone—as if that person had taken up residence in your psyche and was observing and approving of your behavior. Catalogue your interior feelings. Are you more relaxed than normal? Less self-critical? Less stressed? More patient? Does it make any difference to you at all? I would be surprised if it does not.

Now, spend the following fifteen minutes holding the image of someone you feel intimidated or critically evaluated by. Imagine that this person is scrutinizing everything you do, cataloging and judging each error. Which interior state feels most familiar? To what degree might you have previously internalized the attitudes of one or the other? Review those judgments, and if they are negative, can you now, as an adult, defend yourself successfully against them? Catalogue the differences among your feelings with each witness in your mind's eye.

Notice any physical sensations accompanying the recall of each of these people. Does your stomach feel different? Do you have tension in the corners of your lips? Consider how useful it might be to review your interior inhabitants from a detached, objective point of view instead of being uncritically bound to their judgments, requiring their approval, smothered by their excuses for you, or incessantly arguing with them.

STAGE FRIGHT

If the idea of public speaking unnerves you, you have plenty of company: addressing a crowd of strangers is one of the most common phobias among Western European people and is estimated to affect 75 percent of the population. It even has its own medical designations: *anthropophobia* or *glossophobia*. People who can address a crowd with brio and confidence do so because they feel supported from within, confident that they will be able to win the affection of the crowd. However, nothing is *always* one way or another. Sometimes sociopaths have these skills because their self-image is not dependent on any outside source and they have practiced *mimicking* empathy and compassion as a strategy for manipulating others.

Enjoyment is infectious. An individual who takes the stage expecting to have a good time relaxes the audience so they can enjoy *themselves*. Audiences *want* you to win. There is nothing more painful than observing a truly frightened or embarrassed performer onstage. It is an excruciating experience, and audiences dread it. Audiences can watch an accomplished actor express the same feelings with perfect fidelity because they have confidence that the actor or actress is not actually suffering. However, the humiliation of an ordinary person is too painful to bear. Remembering to enjoy yourself with a crowd always imparts an advantage to a performer or public speaker. Here are a couple of tricks that will facilitate that enjoyment.

IDENTIFYING THE DEMON

I purloined the outline of this exercise from neuro-linguistic programming and have used it to help people conquer stage fright. Imagine giving a speech from a stage to a large room full of strangers. If you get the "flutters" search the first several rows carefully. There will be someone in the audience of whom you're afraid or before whose judgments you become anxious and insecure. Find and identify that person. It may be a parent, teacher, sister or brother, an aunt or uncle. Your first task is to identify them and realize that they have always been "in the house": that you've carried them with you for years. Next, try to *determine their age*. Are they the age you might see them today? Older? Younger? Delve as deeply as you can to discover the first instance when that fear was inculcated in you and check their age again. Were they as they appear now? I doubt it.

Now calculate what age *you* were when *they* were the age they appear to be in your mind's eye. For most people it is usually between six or seven and twelve or thirteen—a very impressionable period.

After making that determination, roll time forward in your mind's eye and advance them to the age they would be today. Does seeing them at their current age still unnerve you? If so, move them to the back of the room and see if their influence over you diminishes. If not, strip the scene of all color, and turn it into black and white. If that fails, banish them from the audience altogether. Send them to the lobby, or seat them permanently on a Greyhound bus to nowhere. There's no need for you to remain haunted any longer, and you won't be once you've consciously broken the habit of responding to their appearance in your personal auditorium.

With fear of this intimidating critic removed, now begin an inventory: Are you standing, walking, and dressing in such a way as to defend yourself against this person or delighting in the memory of a loving gaze? Do you highlight the parts of your body of which you're proud and diminish the ones of which you're embarrassed? Can you verbalize what you're doing to yourself—slowing down enough to unpack your motives for choosing costumes more precisely than "this looks good (or bad)"—to include what images and emotions "looking good" and "looking bad" bring to mind?

I'm not suggesting that the desire to look good is neurotic or in any way negative. I am suggesting that a perfectly healthy instinct can disguise aspects of ourselves that are mixed or negative, and the clearer we can be about our own motives, the less conflict we'll experience.

To accomplish practices like these, we must develop our *intention* to do it. We accomplish this in the same way we go to the gym, take the time to jog, help our children with homework, quit smoking, or change any deleterious habit. We *begin*! We take the first step and, most important, *persist* until we build a new habit. I've read that it takes twenty-eight days to do this.

There is no free lunch. No single workshop, guided meditation, weekend retreat, or self-help book will stabilize change in our psyches without personal physical commitment—a rest-of-your-life commitment. All the above may give you good talking points at parties or the coffee shop, but they'll just be talking points, not liberation, not freedom, not the training of the mind and body to be able to withstand sudden impulses and discomforts.

If we are patient, persistent, and consistent we will discover layers of masks disguising our inner narratives, making them appear "real" to us. With awareness and identification—which is to say, becoming conscious—each one's hold on our imaginations becomes more tenuous. Eventually the narratives, disguises, and justifications become boring and fall away of their own accord.

Personal experience has borne this out for me. It requires time and practice to relax the body deeply enough to empty its storage compartments. Once consciously examined, the adhesive grip of false assumptions and ideas is nullified. We reap the benefit of the liberated energy, clarity, and fearlessness previously dedicated to ensuring that such feelings remain isolated from our awareness. No matter what the particulars of your discoveries may be, eventually you will clarify for yourself how, like all humans, you have ascribed fixed and permanent qualities to a self that can neither be located and grasped nor described.

There's absolutely nothing wrong with wanting to look one's best or choosing flattering clothing, but if you are driven to make selections by negative fantasies or archaic fears, it means that you're chained to those fantasies and fears, and it would be useful to drag such feelings from the shadows and befriend, tame, or abandon them.

Imagine the scene again and ask yourself if you would feel the same way if you were wearing a mask. Would a fat belly or heavy thighs that were not "yours" be less disturbing? Do you force yourself to "own" the body you judge negatively by fixing these negative associations as unchangeable attributes of your identity? Can you regard the body parts and your feelings about them as separate entities? Can you imagine how someone else might feel about them? If you can, you are no longer in your actual body but traveling in imaginary terrain and mistaking the map for the territory. This always causes difficulty.

Both masks and meditation can teach us the art of disengaging from such inhibiting fantasies. The point of such reflections is to rest intimately with our self-awareness and the constellations of habits and prejudgments animating our emotions. Once they are visible, practice unpacking and disentangling them, analyzing them carefully. Are they you or are they habits? Are they things you've been told about yourself and believed? If you review them meticulously and skeptically enough, you may realize that what you are identifying as yourself is an amalgamation of habitual thoughts, implications, responses, attitudes, awareness, and sensation without any center at all. If there's no "there" there, what prevents you from putting them in a brown paper bag and leaving them on a bus? What prevents you from changing to be more as you would enjoy being? Setting aside some time every day to do this by meditating is the surest way to ensure that we don't skirt the task.

A PARABLE

Two more months raced by, and the house was assuming its final shape. The biggest boulders had been fitted as foundation stones and chipped away to accommodate the eccentric rock shapes of the next course. The Lone Ranger had to admit being impressed by the Buddha's ability to chip here and chip there and fit the stones together so snugly he could not fit a knife blade between them. "My gosh," he thought, "a white man could live in this house."

It was a limpid, cool evening after a long day, and the Lone Ranger, Tonto, and the Buddha were relaxing. Buddha was washing their dishes, and the Lone Ranger was shocked when he noticed a folded stack of his clothes—all expertly cleaned and repaired. "They're like new," he'd whispered to Tonto. "These Orientals—it's a natural ability."

"French weave," the Buddha said, as he handed Tonto his cleaned and repaired shirt.

When their tobacco ran out, Tonto taught the Lone Ranger how to pick, dry, and smoke kinnikinnick, the Indian tobacco. That night's dinner had been a brace of quail he'd trapped with a clever twig snare. "By God, he is really pulling his weight," the Lone Ranger thought. He tried to remember if Tonto had exhibited these skills in any episodes they'd done together and reflected how interesting they might have been, especially to kids. This occurred to him with a twinge of regret.

Tonto had constructed a little sweat lodge, making a frame of bent willows and covering it with many layers of dried grass. The Lone Ranger had to admit that when he stepped out of it, he felt clean from the pores out, though the lodge used almost no water. The Buddha had joined them and said he was extremely impressed by it. Tonto had also created a little corn, beans, and squash garden patch, which was doing well, the beans growing upward using the corn stalks for support and the squash, rolling down the mounds of earth that had been raised for the corn. "This is the life," the Lone Ranger thought, surveying the camp as if it were his plantation.

The Buddha wiped his hands and asked the Lone Ranger, "What's that mask made of?"

The Ranger replied, "The finest pima cotton."

The Buddha asked, "Do you ever take it off?"

"I can't," he responded.

"What do you mean?" Buddha asked.

"I've worn it so many years that it's kind of stuck to my face. A doctor thought it might be a kind of fungus. But I'm totally fine with it. I told you once, I know who the Lone Ranger is so it's easy for me to be him all the time.

Turning to Tonto, the Buddha inquired, "Have you ever seen his face?"

"Not in many years," Tonto replied diffidently. "When he washed the mask, he used to put a bag over his head while it was drying in case his face fell off."

"You're kidding me." The Buddha laughed and, turning to the Lone Ranger, asked, "Why did you do that?"

"Because when the mask was off, things could get confusing. I had no idea who I was," the Lone Ranger replied candidly. "Just another out-of-work actor without purpose. When I'm the Lone Ranger, I know who I am and what I'm doing."

The Buddha inquired, "And what is that exactly?"

"I fight evil."

No sooner than the words were out of his mouth, a gigantic, seven-headed cobra appeared in front of him, each head a snarling wolf. The Lone Ranger drew both guns like lightning and fired them, one after the other, each heavy silver bullet disintegrating a wolf's head off the monstrous cobra's trunk.

The Buddha clapped appreciatively like a young child. "Do it again. That was wonderful."

"Well, I'd need another serpent," the Lone Ranger said diffidently, and immediately a duplicate appeared, snarling and howling, and the Lone Ranger repeated his performance.

"That was great," the Buddha said sincerely. The Lone Ranger never thought to inquire how the cobras had materialized.

Tonto regarded the Buddha seriously and said, "You're scarin' the crap outta me, Buddha."

"You ain't seen nothin' yet," Buddha replied, grinning, and held up his right hand with the fingers extended. At the tip of each finger, a tiny cobra bearing five miniature wolf heads appeared, each head rendering "Tumblin' Tumbleweeds," in wolf howls all singing together in harmony.

Scout whinnied, and from far away a nearly inaudible whinny floated through the limpid air in response.

Trying to distract the Buddha from any more tricks, Tonto jerked a thumb in Scout's direction and said, "Bait a trap with pussy, and you'll catch Scout every time."

Buddha laughed. "I wouldn't know about that, Tonto."

Under the influence of vigorous physical work, the health of the Lone Ranger and Tonto has improved and their energy has risen. The Lone Ranger is beginning to notice the selfless activity of the Buddha but still filters it through his ancient prejudices. Tonto is settling into his older cultural wisdom, grounding himself in the familiar and the sensible. The Lone Ranger tiptoes into this first discussion of his identity.

PART TWO

Keeping Your
Learning Accessible

"Getting out of my own way" has always been the hard part. My own "mask," my natural face, which protects me from risk and vulnerability, shifts the focus to me, rather than channeling it toward the character I am trying to bring to life. The result is that while many of my reads are decent, too few are spectacular, and most are not personally satisfying. What a difference a few hours can make! Through the simple act of putting on a neutral mask (literally), I found I was able to lose myself and live through the character—simply, honestly, authentically, and with a sense of ease that I have rarely experienced.

JULIE MOYLAN, VOICETRAX STUDENT

9
The Devil You Know

It's important to be clear that emotions and ideas of a unique self are an integral part of our human inheritance. It is not a neurotic failing to have an ego or a sense of oneself as an isolated organism. For his part, the Buddha refused to answer the question of whether or not the ego existed; it was beside the point. Usually when we describe someone as egocentric, we are criticizing self-centered behavior. Such behavior is the expression of an ego that has never perceived what might be called objective reality, which in its essence, is impersonal. However, the ego is useful to us or it would never have survived the crucible of evolution. It guides us to eat well, brush our teeth, behave socially, think strategically and defensively, and protect our bodies. It helps us to plan ahead and gives us a comprehensible matrix through which we can understand others.

The ego has a shadow side we ignore at our peril. It may assert its preeminence by competition, promoting its own well-being at the expense of others, misreading objective facts and confusing them with its desires, laying claim to goods and services far beyond any need for them, and indulging the impulse to satisfy its every whim. Furthermore, the ego tends to privilege its own thoughts and feelings. However, buried beneath consciousness, the ego's judgments and selections remain directly related to our ideas of who we are. Those thoughts and feelings that are acceptable to our 'small mind,' our personality we accept; the others we reject. This sort of small-mind selection process is, when we examine it more closely, completely arbitrary. It is the self that likes or dislikes, is attracted to or fears its various thoughts and impulses. One of my teachers, in describing this condition, once said, "There's no feeling that's crazy. Feeling something and not *wanting* to feel it is crazy."

It is our unquestioned *attachment* to the ego that transforms it from a useful ally into a demanding warden. Sometimes we attach it to a group—a team, state, nation, and so forth. By willingly identifying with larger entities, we garner an expanded, more powerful sense of who we are. This is often a by-product of feeling separate from the rest of the universe, impossibly tiny against its immensity. After all, if we imagine ourselves as *not* everything else, we diminish ourselves to the point of disappearing.

It's a misunderstanding to believe that the object of meditation is to obliterate the ego and thereby achieve some imagined unalterable state of bliss. Such thoughts are flypaper for the unwary or what Gary Snyder once referred to as "sexless nirvana."

Elevating the self to primary importance (perhaps humanity's most persistent delusion) has a shadow—the generation of ceaseless anxiety because it is so at odds with the extrapersonal ways in which the universe so visibly operates that self-promoting endeavors are repeatedly dashed against the rocks of fact.

It is a common strategy of a narcissist to befriend others who, like himself, consider themselves to be elite or entitled. Approbation from such self-important others bolsters the narcissist's delusion that they are special. I'm reminded of this when I visit the offices of politicians and celebrities, clustered with photographs of them chumming with other famous people. Such photos always make me imagine a *New Yorker* cartoon with a thought balloon over the subject's head exclaiming, "See, I AM special! I'm with *them*." We're all unique but not necessarily special.

Conveniently omitted from such vanity is the reality that the entire universe—including the self—changes constantly. In the next ten minutes, Mr. or Ms. Magnificent could be captured on an iPhone picking their nose or uttering a banality. Today's friend may be tomorrow's persecutor. Nothing in the realm of human affairs can be pinned down with absolute certainty, least of all our own bodies, which—despite our fervent wishes and application of expensive products to slow aging and smooth the furrows time scores in our brows—defy us by changing. We cannot prevent our lives from ending. To this point, one of Suzuki-roshi's book of lectures was entitled *Not Always So.*

Our ideas about who we are may offer us temporary comforts and the illusion of stability but are no more a defense against change than sandcastles erected to block the tides. One definition of sanity and contentment is learning to exist with the universe as it is or, to put it in one of Suzuki-roshi's favorite phrases, *things as it is.* (I originally considered his confusion of tense between the noun and pronoun as his problem with English but later understood the deeper significance that all things are part of one big thing.) This "one big thing" sometimes confuses those who believe that Buddhists are atheists. While normally we do not believe in a creator separate from the rest of his or her works, it would not be misleading to suggest that each and every particle of creation is a divine oracle of the inexpressible.

Believing everything we think creates difficulty for us in the same way believing there is an internal entity within us does. If we could observe our thoughts with the detachment of a movie, or in the way we watch clouds transform themselves from camels to turbaned genies to mountain ranges, no single thought would be overly problematic.

Without attaching to them and taking them as either real or unreal, each can be understood as a projection on the screen of our awareness, an expression or mask of emptiness. In the absence of a physical, permanent ego, self-awareness can be conceived as a cluster of distinct, separate awarenesses of our eyes, ears, nose, mouth, body, and mind—each of which, according to Buddhist philosophy, possess its own consciousness.

MEDITATION AND THERAPY

Thirty minutes of daily meditation is roughly equivalent to a weekly therapy session of three and a half hours, with the added benefit of not having to wait a week to review an important point that arose during the prior session. However, as I noted earlier, meditation will not solve or cure every problem, and it's important to understand that psychological therapy can be extremely useful.

Somewhere I once read that "psychology is the compassion of the West," and that made sense to me. At the time I began my study of Zen, I'd made the decision to stop using heroin, and I undertook concentrated work with two psychiatrists (the first died midtreatment) to understand the roots of my self-medication and desire to keep myself asleep. Therapy was helpful to me in taming the junkyard dog ravaging my psyche. At the same time, I began practicing at the San Francisco Zen Center and began learning, through meditation, how to remain present when difficult thoughts and emotions arose, and this certainly facilitated my therapy. Throughout my adult life, into my late sixties, I would check in with a favorite therapist from time to time just to ensure that I was not deceiving myself—something I was once very skilled at.

The primary difference between meditation and therapy, as I've come to understand them, is that a therapist attempts to teach the patient's ego to perceive and respond to the world more objectively and to be less trapped by neurotic, inappropriate trains of thought. The therapist also models such behavior for them. If a person is stuck in a problematic mental loop, the therapist offers an alternative, more objective view. If trust develops between them, the patient may begin to reassess his choices, first by asking himself, "What would Doctor So-and-So say?" As time passes and their relationship deepens, a successful conclusion might be described as the patient absorbing (introjecting in psych-speak) the doctor's more objective view of the world. I have, on occasion, referred troubled Zen students to therapists for problems that needed to be resolved before they could effectively practice meditation.

Dainin Katagiri-roshi, a Soto Zen master who came to America to help Suzuki-roshi before founding his own Zen practice center in Minnesota, once said that Zen practice was like putting your life in a bamboo tube. "Even if you're crazy, the craziness is in the tube, too, so it's all right." Meditation, psychedelics, and masks offer us the experience of temporarily being *without* a dominant and demanding ego. In such a state, we are flooded with new data and information, that often even out our neurotic impulses and thoughts.

In terms of these masks and games, meditation helps us with securing our insights permanently. Without intending to demote psychology, there is a clear distinction between adjusting a self to the world and an awareness that is not mediated by a self.

There is no guarantee that our habitual self perceives reality without distortion. Desires, old angers, and delusions or past traumas can dye or reframe our perception to such a degree that we cannot respond to fresh circumstances and often force them into previously created molds. Buddhist psychology names such powerful emotions *kleshas*—negative mental states that cloud the mind's original clarity and manifest themselves as unwholesome actions. This is an important distinction. When we search for liberation or freedom, we are not searching for anything foreign to us or an external power that we must find and possess. We are simply clearing away the dead leaves and brambles so that the flowers of consciousness can blossom unimpeded.

These kleshas are universal to humans and obscure our original, enlightened nature. Such difficulties arrive with every human, whose birth is a link in an endless chain of desires and actions that led to his or her creation.

It is easy to forget that we humans are like flesh radios tuned to the "human" frequency. The content of our thoughts and feelings may be personal, but the underlying emotions are universal. We *all* know anger, despite being triggered by different causes and expressing it in different ways. We all understand joy, happiness, fear, and awe, but each will be generated by different circumstances and expressed in a uniquely personal fashion.

To the extent that we do not believe that our own inner life includes the potential to be cruel, competitive, envious, hateful, or even murderous, we pose a danger to ourselves and others. The fixed assumption that "we are good" lulls us to believe that we are immune to the errors of others whom we designate as evil. Such a belief exempts us from any need to monitor ourselves and remain on guard to censor negative impulses *when* (not if) they arise. It is more comforting to preordain that we are good and cease self-examination because then, when destructive events occur, it must be the fault of those evil others. This is a dangerous simplification arising directly from the fixed ideas we hold about ourselves.

A PARABLE

Weeks later, the Buddha, Tonto, and the Lone Ranger were gathered around a small morning fire. Tonto had just finished his sun salutations and prayers. Buddha was slurping a bowl of nettles. His hummingbird friend was perched on the bowl's rim, sampling the soup and singing, "I dream of Jeannie with the light-brown folks," in the voice of an old Mississippi Delta bluesman.

Tonto sat beside the Lone Ranger, who was taking pieces of a rabbit off a spit. Tonto had called it in by blowing through a piece of grass stretched between his thumbs and the heels of his hands. As they began to eat, Buddha placed his hands together as if praying and muttered a chant over the rabbit's body.

"He can't hear you now, Buddy-Boy," the Lone Ranger chuckled, ripping off a haunch.

"How would you know?" Buddha asked, unperturbed.

"'Cause he's dead. Anyone can see that."

"When a tree falls down in the forest, is it dead?" Buddha inquired innocently.

The Lone Ranger thought a moment. "Well, not immediately."

"Okay," Buddha replied. "How do you know when it IS dead?"

The Lone Ranger appeared puzzled.

Indicating the rabbit, Buddha said, "If you can't answer that, you can't assure me that the rabbit is completely dead either. But since you're eating him, you might just thank him for the gift of his body."

"It wasn't a gift," the Lone Ranger said. "Tonto trapped it."

Tonto said, "I didn't trap him. He came to me when I called—it was a gift."

"Don't correct me in front of strangers," the Lone Ranger hissed.

Buddha returned to his chanting. The rabbit turned his fully charred head in the Buddha's direction and whispered, "Can you believe this shit?"

The Lone Ranger's prejudices and beliefs are highlighted here. Like most Westerners, he behaves as if the products of Earth are provided solely for his use. His ideas of life and death are unexamined, as are his ideas of reciprocity. These assumptions make up the cultural heritage of Western Caucasians, and few are free of them. All cultures have some variants. Considering the ravages humans have perpetuated on Earth and on one another—the massive extractions of all sorts; the clear-cuts; the dams; the pollutants in air, soil, and water; and the prejudices and horrors that we have *tolerated*—is to understand that we ourselves are not so different from the Lone Ranger. To the degree that we use products created by this castaway economy, we are responsible for it. How many of us, for instance, can be *certain* that the production of our "clean" computers and smartphones do no harm to the planet or the people who produce them? We don't know because we don't have to know, and knowing could be inconvenient. I recently saw a documentary film that showed mountains being blown apart to extract the crystals required for computer chips, in precisely the same manner that our old economy blew mountaintops apart to claim the coal inside them. We are not so different from the Lone Ranger. We are all entwined, and there is no pure place to stand outside all of it.

10
Masked in a Hall of Mirrors

*In thinking about the mask exercise[s], it was a little scary
and amazing how completely I felt my personality being set
aside in favor of the persona from the mask. . . . It was
primal and brought a fresh truth to each question and
feeling. It gave me the feeling of completely inhabiting
another person.*

RONI GALLIMORE, WORKSHOP PARTICIPANT

It is not the case that a mask is false and that which it covers is real.
A mask is a physical object that actually exists. Both the mask and the
human face coexist simultaneously, but only one at a time is visible, like
the shift of focus between a dream and the dreamer. If the self is not a
discrete entity, isn't it possible to consider our notions about it a mask?

The self is an *awareness* offering us survival efficiencies—a stream-
lining of decisions, for instance, a focus for the body in space, memory,
and emotions. It is like the armature in a sculpture around which the
clay is fashioned; except that, in the case of the self, there is nothing we
can isolate or grasp. In the same way we might regard physical objects
as masks of the universal formless energy of which everything is composed, we can say that the self is a convenient mask for the cluster of
sense organs and awareness we think of as ourselves.

Having said that, there are often situations when we do not want the distractions and limits of self-absorption intruding, particularly when we are solving complex problems or executing critical procedures, acting quickly and intuitively in the moment, or seeking deep intimacy with others—as a brain surgeon, warrior, hunter, or lover.

If there is no physical captain perceiving and expressing our beliefs, we are freer to regard them as temporary masks or filters that facilitate our comprehension of our unfathomable world; but though these beliefs are temporary or provisional, that does not mean they are false. Such expressions are like dreams of a purer world we act out with our bodies. Dreams are real things.

While most people do not take their nighttime dreams literally, it is a nearly universal practice to parse and analyze their details. When we wake, memory of the previous night's dream may vanish completely or leave only a trace, but who would argue that the dreamer experienced nothing? The solidities and certainties of waking life are curiously altered in dreams, reminding us of the fluidity at the core of our ideas about reality. The dream world, though exempt from ordinary rules, always feels real. In dreams, our awareness traverses many of the same journeys, experiences, sense impressions, and plays of sensation and emotions as it does when we are awake.

The energy made visible by the mask of self is the same formlessness or emptiness presented by every other mask—our original universal denominator. We cannot perceive emptiness directly but know it by intuition and observation of its infinite variety of expression as forms. If emptiness had any fixed foundational structure, it would be limited in its expression, and so we can deduce from the plentitude of forms in the universe how unbounded it is. We believe we know the self because we have constructed it meticulously over time, piecing together information we've been told about ourselves and deduced for ourselves from the responses of others to us and our own impulses and habits until it has become a fixture of consciousness. Its original limitless dimensions have been reduced to manageable attributes.

This is the reason why the Lone Ranger will say to the Buddha at one point, "Without my mask, I don't know who I am." Since we can't locate the self nor determine its properties, the self is equivalent to a *fixed idea*—like a snapshot of a flowing river. We have all participated in the construction of the self since infancy—in our captain's cabin decorating its walls with snapshots and Post-it Notes.

Herodotus observed that "you can never step into the same river twice," but a photograph remains unchanged. Perhaps this accounts for much of the despair experienced by people struggling with compulsive behaviors or chronic depression. Part of what makes their efforts so persistently difficult is that their problematic behaviors and moods have been scored into the brain by repetition, like runnels of water scoring a dirt hillside. These behaviors have, through repetition and practice, become an integral part of that person's physical architecture until they are assumed to be permanent qualities. Nonetheless, they are little more than habits, however deep and obdurate. As beings assembled of emptiness, with a fluid, constantly changing brain, we are capable of altering the most entrenched behaviors.

Addicts have stopped stepping into the river. They are habitually revisiting or protecting old wounds and frozen beliefs and therefore retriggering their old defenses. Deciding who we are, making of ourselves a finished project, cinches our attachment to time and therefore to dying and all its attendant anxieties. It indicates that we've abandoned the surprises, uncertainties, and ceaseless change of the present moment, where our life actually takes place, for the false certainties of the measurable, the known, and previously experienced.

A fixed decision of "who we are" is like condemning ourselves to live in a large, complex museum. At some point, no matter how large and interesting it may be, its fixed dimensions will have been thoroughly explored and the possibility of novelty and surprise eradicated. Once that occurs, life loses its savor and luster. We either lie (to keep things interesting) or seek the stimulation of drugs, alcohol, adrenaline, or personal dramas to ward off depression and boredom. When those strategies fail (and they do) a loss of joie de vivre and a descent into cynicism and sometimes suicide may follow.

Some people discuss knowing oneself as if the self was a finite body of knowledge that could be mastered, like memorizing the Torah or the Koran. Such a statement is meant to signify wisdom, but is "knowing oneself" a provable assertion? If we accept that the self is interdependent with oxygen, sunshine, microbes in the soil that produce our food, pollinating insects, and so forth, it becomes clear that the self cannot possibly be a separate, independent entity. This is why it's more accurate to represent the self as a mask of formlessness—what Buddhists refer to as emptiness. Such a shift of focus liberates us to regard ourselves and the rest of creation as unique, unrepeatable expressions of a common force—a continually refreshed kaleidoscope. Attaching *only* to ourselves as a fixed self is the delusion.

🌀 🌀 🌀

There is an engaging exchange about the self in Carlos Castaneda's book *Journey to Ixtlan*. The conversation takes place between Castaneda and the Yaqui* shaman Don Juan Matus, who has been training Castaneda to perceive the world as a sorcerer does, urging him to "erase his personal history."

> "Take yourself for instance," he went on saying. "Right now you don't know whether you are coming or going [with me]. And that is so, because I have erased my personal history. I have, little by little, created a fog around me and my life. And now nobody knows for sure who I am or what I do."
>
> "But, you yourself know who you are, don't you?" I interjected.
>
> "You bet I . . . don't," he exclaimed and rolled on the floor, laughing at my surprised look. . . .

---

*The Yaqui are an Aztecan ethnic group in the valley of the Río Yaqui in Sonora, Mexico, and the southwestern United States. They have communities in Chihuahua, Durango, and Sinaloa, Mexico, and in Tucson, Arizona, California, Texas, and Nevada.

"This is the little secret I'm going to give to you today," he said in a low voice. "Nobody knows my personal history. Nobody knows who I am or what I do. Not even I." . . .

"How can I know who I am?" he said, sweeping the surroundings with a gesture of his head. . . .

"Little by little you must create a fog around yourself; you must erase everything around you until nothing can be taken for granted, until nothing is any longer for sure, or real. Your problem now is that you're too real. Your endeavors are too real; your moods are too real. Don't take things so for granted." . . .

"You see," he went on, "we only have two alternatives; we either take everything for sure and real, or we don't. If we follow the first, we end up bored to death with ourselves and with the world. If we follow the second and erase personal history, we create a fog around us, a very exciting and mysterious state in which nobody knows where the rabbit will pop out, not even ourselves."[1]

Don Juan's vocabulary and metaphors are indigenous to his shamanic tradition, but his description of reality is fairly equivalent to Buddhist iconography, with the *tonal* equating with form and the *nagual* similar to the Buddhist notion of emptiness. The tonal represents every object that can be recognized and named in normal reality. It is like a table set with all the things of the world on it. The nagual is the space surrounding the table. It is the undefined area where magic (for instance) can exist and where the certainties of the tonal no longer exist. For Don Juan, the sole thing we can control is the commitment to follow "a path with a heart." Buddhists would call it intention and the path itself compassion.

Our human mask is no less real than anything else. It is our fate for this lifetime, and though we may change masks, permanent existence without *any* mask is not an option in this world of form. We can visit the empty kingdom from time to time but are forbidden to reside there until we are ready to give up this body.

Buddhism is not the only path to knowledge—neither is Don Juan's way, LSD, ayahuasca, fasting, prayer, or worship. Each has a transcendental truth within it and is worthy of deep study, but flitting among them, trying first one and then another, discourages depth and condemns us to the superficiality of water striders, the long-legged bugs who travel on the surface tension of streams. Experiment all you like, but once you've found a path, it's important to stick to it if you intend depth.

I chose Buddhism more than forty years ago, and my teacher has transmitted his authority to me to teach and ordain priests. I would never assert that mine is the best or only path or even that it is for everyone. Sometimes I think that Zen is such a strict path that no ordinary, happy person would come to it willingly. That said, I can certify from personal experience that it is practical and useful in alleviating suffering, producing clarity, and promoting fearlessness and kindness, and as far as I can determine, it has no deleterious side effects except, in some instances, that of proselytizing. Numerous paths have a heart, but to decide which one to follow, we have to honestly question ourselves and then heed the answer.

As a child, my father cautioned me repeatedly that "life is short," and in the expanse of youthful days I anticipated, I never understood what he meant. I do now. At a few months shy of eighty, I attend and officiate funerals with increasing regularity, and each reminds me, as do my daily meditations and personal diminishments, that for impermanent beings "hunted by death," as Don Juan puts it, there is only time to make choices, strategize, and follow the path dictated by our intention. That is the law of the human world. Warriors—men and women who stand up for what they believe—understand this as well. They make commitments and abide by them. Those who follow paths without a heart reap the whirlwind. The problem is, they may take all of us with them.

A PARABLE

That night was calm and cool. The Big Dipper and Venus had risen in the sky, clearly visible over the glow of coals.

The Lone Ranger's personal cottage was complete, even with a cottonwood door studded with homemade nails the Lone Ranger had fashioned in a small clay smelter where he'd melted iron ore. A silhouette of himself on a rearing Silver had been artfully burned into the door.

On his side of camp, Tonto's small garden of corn, beans, and squash was thriving. Once a week, Tonto performed a ceremony, and despite the Lone Ranger's cynicism, a small rain cloud always appeared directly over his crops and watered them. At one end of the garden was a twig pen filled with rabbits and clicking quail.

The Lone Ranger surveyed the scene contentedly and advanced an idea: "Men," he said, "I propose that we divide the night into watches of three hours each."

Buddha said, "Watch what?"

The Lone Ranger looked at him as if he were mad. "All this," he said, indicating the camp, his house, and the nearly finished treasure house—tomb. "We have a very high-end camp here. It's something others might covet."

"They might," said the Buddha, "but that would be their problem. Don't make it yours. You're trying to fix things in place. Never works."

Buddha made a gesture, and the entire desert filled with copies of the Lone Ranger's homestead. "Now everyone can have one," he said.

"Stop fucking around," the Lone Ranger said with some pique. "I know what's true." He pointed up at the North Star. "That doesn't move," he said. "Right, Tonto?"

Tonto shrugged, "Not in my lifetime anyway."

"Perhaps not from here it doesn't," the Buddha responded, "but if we looked at it from a point in the Big Dipper it might." He immediately transported their collective awareness to the star Dubhe,

at the tip of the Big Dipper's ladle. "Polaris is over there," the Buddha indicated and then whipped them back to Earth. "Polaris rests in the line with the celestial North Pole; that's why it doesn't appear to move. But it moves, LR. Everything moves. Don't be confused."

The Lone Ranger said, "We don't need it anymore, Buddy-Boy. We have compasses, accurate watches to calculate distance. We've mapped the entire globe. Hell, they got GPS gizmos that'll show a Pakistani cab driver how to drive around LA. We always know where we are."

The Buddha slurped his nettles. "By the way," he said idly, "who's 'we'?"

The Lone Ranger slapped his chest. "People. Me."

"You told me once," Buddha continued, smiling pleasantly, "that without your mask you didn't know who you were. So . . . ," he paused to wipe a fleck of nettle off a tooth, "if you don't know who you are, how can you know where you are?"

The Lone Ranger regarded him steadily and with perhaps a tad of malevolence.

Tonto bit off a chunk of rabbit. "That's just wordplay, right?"

The Buddha held up his hand. "Are you chewing a word?"

Tonto thought about that for a moment and then pointed at the rabbit and said, "Tehahonhtané:ken. That's rabbit in my language."

"What about the word I," Buddha continued. "Can you point to that?"

The coals twinkled, and puffs of wood gas flickered over their surface like miniature northern lights. While Tonto considered what the Buddha had said, Buddha pulled his right foot onto his thigh and placed his hands in his lap, the back of one hand resting inside the palm of the other, thumbs forming a round circle. He lowered his eyes and remained upright and still, breathing quietly. After a while, Tonto kicked off his moccasins, crossed his legs, and followed Buddha's example.

The Lone Ranger kept looking up at the North Star, cocking his head one way and then another, looking at the Buddha and then back to the sky. He smoothed a patch of earth in front of himself, picked up a twig, and sketched a number of circles that appeared to represent the relationship between Earth, the moon, and several stars. He studied it for some time, comparing his sketches with the lofty model above his head, and then he walked back to his saddlebags and retrieved a telescope and extended it to regard the moon.

Noticing this, the Buddha said, "Isn't it funny how the entire moon can fit into that little tube?"

The Buddha is beginning to push the Lone Ranger and Tonto harder, to confront ideas and concepts that appear true but are actually beliefs. Tonto is willing to think about such things; the Lone Ranger is still in the realm of constructing physical models to prove or disprove his own observations.

11
More on Meditation
and Masks

For many years, even during my young adulthood, my thoughts and emotions were in turmoil, as if I were locked in a closet with my violent and hypercritical father. I was subject to deep depressions, which often induced a sense of hopelessness, and nearly constant anger; a state of mind that I sought relief from with heroin. My father was an omnipresent distraction, intruding on many decisions and my self-regard. I was forced to contend with him daily. Within a year of sitting zazen, I began to feel that the door of our mutual closet had sprung ajar, admitting some light and fresh air, indicating an escape route. Now, many years later, though aspects of my father's problematic personality arise from time to time, my experience of him today is more analogous to our hiking independently in Yosemite and catching sight of one another from time to time. In the absence of daily pressure, it has become much easier to remember his generosity, brilliance, and fearlessness and be happy seeing him and remembering his often wise counsel.

Meditation is thousands of years old, older even than Buddhism, and probably has its roots in the most ancient practices of hunter-gatherer societies. Observe a stork or a frog hunting in perfect stillness. Early man noticed these teachers and imitated them. Inuit people today hunt seals by chopping a small breathing hole into the ice and sitting before it, absolutely immobile and fully alert, until the moment when the seal rises for air and they harpoon it. Traditionally, seals are a source of nourishment, and the Inuit use their fat in tiny stoves and as candles. Any movement or failure of attention and their source of food, warmth, and light could be lost. Meditation is practiced in some manner or another by virtually every culture and religion on Earth because it is so effective at dissolving rigid boundaries between self and other.

We don't meditate to shut down our thinking (death will take care of that), to wallow in introspection, or simply to chill. If you can't be at ease with your thoughts as you are right now, trying to relax in your usual state won't convey many benefits. To acquire a clearer view, we observe ourselves, our bodies and feelings: Are we trying to maintain certain situations as permanent? Are we in the grip of powerful desires or emotions? Are we in physical pain or despair? The root cause of our unhappiness eventually reveals itself, and we can then just drop those destructive preconceptions and emotions like bad habits.

When we are hooked by a powerful emotion, we're like a swimmer in a strong riptide, preoccupied with the struggle to escape. When we can perceive what we're feeling from a detached point of view—noticing where in the body the emotion is located, what particular part of the narrative has the most impact on us, what details are fueling our emotions—the force of this current weakens. Also, the more persistently we meditate, the more confidence we build in *nirodha* and our understanding that meditation and mindfulness can contain whatever arises without destroying our equilibrium; we can endure even painful situations more impersonally. These are the first steps toward coming to terms with the fluidity of the ego.

These benefits all derive from regular meditation—keeping a daily appointment to meet ourselves without distractions. If you fix a time to sit every day and stick to it, you will have taken the first step toward controlling your twenty-four hours. Many people accept exercise as a daily necessity for good health, and many would rehearse job-related skills and important events, from weddings to presidential debates, to ensure optimum performance. How many of us reserve the time to practice intimacy with our own bodies and minds on a daily basis?

FORMAL PRACTICE, INFORMAL MIND

The *forms* of Buddhist practice—sitting "just so," bowing, holding the hands in certain mudras—are quite similar to theater games and masks in that they induce us to resist the demands of our monkey mind and to subordinate personal preferences for a more important purpose. By following fixed parameters, whether or not we like them, we trick the self into exposing its predilections by its resistance, and thus we can discover how it controls us and works against our best interests.

The "I" that rebels against form and routine is the "I" causing us problems. The self we honor in every instance is also the one quarreling with a wife or husband, resisting discipline, giving the finger to a rude driver, insisting on things being the way we want. The "I" who can't sit still is the "I" helpless against impulsive action or beliefs or unable to stand firmly enough to defend a perspective in an argument. The "I" who continually frets about being correct or who wants to be the best is the "I" addicted to self-centeredness.

The established norms of Buddhist practice offer us convenient, non-egocentric yardsticks against which to measure our efforts. These methods or forms are not rigid rules but *aids* that offer the meditator an objective standard against which to measure his or her own attentiveness. If we could sit any way we wanted and bow any way we wanted, without a standard, how would we ever know how well we were paying attention? If we could come to the zendo at any time of the day and choose to sit or not sit, how would that teach us self-control? With nothing to resist, the edges of the self would never need to appear.

These forms were not created so that a Buddhist policeman could embarrass us and make us "wrong." They are training aids to practice retraining physical and mental habits. Unless you press against them, you might never notice them. Without a bar to measure the height of our leaps, how could we grade our own efforts? Without a model to imitate, how will we notice where we are missing the mark? A Zen aphorism describes the rationale for this rigor . . .

By practicing repeatedly, sitting quietly with the body and breath, our ancient histories and narratives rise and fall repeatedly until they begin to lose pungency. Before long we become more adept at regarding them as phenomena, with no more substance than a gas, and are able to, at first, discriminate and then disengage habitual emotional responses to them. Deprived of stimulation, the mind slows, and one practices resting in awareness for extended periods of time.

Masks offer a perch similar to the involvement of awareness and attention while meditating—to stand outside (or at least beside) habitual thought processes and so to experience feelings and events that, for myriad reasons, the self may have difficulty accepting.

12
The Masks of Language

We cannot remember our prespeech consciousness because from the moment of birth we were surrounded, enticed, entertained, and educated by humans employing speech to transmit feelings and their reality to us. Through speech, we were, little by little, initiated into a conceptual world, a *description,* which trains us to perceive reality framed and described by that language. Once we can organize these received descriptions on our own as an unbroken continuity, we have achieved full cultural membership. The cost of that membership is expulsion from the Garden of Eden, the precognitive state of unity, and entry into the (relative) knowledge of good and evil—an apt description of a once seemless reality balkanized by language.

On one level, words operate by coding raw experience to create catalogs of known events. These known events become incorporated into the brain's predictive functions—the ability to identify objects from minimal data points. This shorthand has survival benefits, simplifying the brain's work and making rapid decisions easier.

The shadow side of this precious gift is that once things have been named, we no longer inhabit a world renewed moment by moment and refreshed by surprise.

If we extend this examination of language to the subject of the self, we can observe how words like *here, there, up, down, front,* and *behind,* while useful, imply a fixed, permanent point against which direction, space, and time are conceived. As much as these terms locate and guide us for practical problem solving, they also implicitly assure us that we are really here, a fixed identity (moving right along next to our old pal, the Lone Ranger), along with all the other isolated beings and objects in our conceptual universe described by words.

For all its innumerable benefits, language, like everything else, has a shadow side. Words and definitions—useful and necessary as they are—block ancillary, subtle attributes and relationships of named entities from consciousness while privileging publicly agreed-upon denotations. Our training as cultural members is complete only when our common vocabulary consists of definitions and concepts agreed upon by our culture. When they do not match, either communication fails or individuals are forced to invent new expressive forms appropriate to the way they actually perceive. We call such individuals artists, and their work often aids us in expanding our perception.

We don't actually know the new tree in front of us unless we've seen it before, yet we understand that it's a tree. From that generalized understanding, interest in its *particularity* is often diminished. The benefits of such efficiency reduce the need to carefully observe and study each independent thing. Had our ancient ancestors focused all their awareness on the splendor of a butterfly, they might not have retained enough awareness to watch for predators. The tax exacted by this efficiency is that we inhabit a world of sealed definitions, fooling us into feeling that we already know everything.

If we examine the tree deeply, we become less certain about where its "treeness" resides. It is revealed as an entity in flux, interpenetrating (or interbeing) with the rest of the universe. It is *not* simply a cluster of molecules gathered into a sack with the word *tree* stenciled on it. It generates oxygen; holds soil, shelters birds, voles, insects, lichen, and fungus; stores water; and is a food bank for woodpeckers and an area-wide communication network with other trees through root systems and mycelium networks, warning them about pests and illness. All these functions are a *small* part of the numerous aspects of this life-form, which the word *tree* can obscure from our awareness. How easy it then becomes to clear-cut forests to make toilet paper and glossy magazines.

It should be apparent that I am leaning toward describing the word *tree* as a mask. In the same way, our ideas about our self are masks (often multiple masks). Once we've identified and labeled ourselves, we can believe we've figured out who we are and cease exploration and investigation. To say "I know myself" is to photograph a river. The cost of such mental shortcuts is high.

Failing to perceive the fluid, interactive complexity of life because it is camouflaged by language is loss of the world—reducing interdependent, self-organized entities (and their myriad attachments) to a form of chattel. Perhaps it is the diminution of direct experience, of a complex, nuanced, understanding, that is the real villain in humankind's current destruction of the natural world. Isn't it possible that we humans are simply following ancient, unquestioned scripts based on inherited historical realities, assumptions, and customs and protected from critical reexamination by the shadow of language? I offer the feeble human response to the existential threat of global warming as a case in point.

As T. S. Eliot once said, and Robert Creeley repeated in one of his poems, "I gotta use words when I talk to you." Words are what we have, and because we are forced to use them, we must use them carefully and continually refresh and clarify them so that their definitions are clear, current, and useful. Consider charged terms like *liberal, conservative, right wing, progressive,* used and defined oppositely according to one's political agenda and beliefs. When words are used so inappropriately, are they descriptive of anything? They have been reconfigured as weapons and now organize and mobilize millions of people and generate hours of discourse producing rancor and discord—while the world burns and our fellow creatures disappear by the millions.

Thousands of years ago in the *Analects,* Confucius wrestled with the problem of language. He concluded that "the degeneration of public discourse was preceded, and caused by, the erosion of private discourse."[1]

Another way to say this is that when we speak unconsciously, we forget that words have shadows, and one shadow is their reduction of complexity. The second shadow is that words are totally dependent on the *intention* we harness them to serve. Navigating this terrain requires intuition and empathy as a constant corrective. In a tough 2018 run-off election in Mississippi, a white congresswoman, who was running against a black competitor, complimented a high-status white supporter by saying, "If he invited me to a public hanging, I'd be on the front row." At best, the congresswoman was blind to her state's dark history as a leader in extrajudicial murders in United States with 581 *known* lynchings of African Americans between 1882 and 1968 and certainly unaware of the anxiety such a remark might arouse in African Americans. At worst, she was deliberately reinjecting an image and idea into public discourse that should never get past anyone's lips.

Meditation is a specific antidote to such word-lock, giving us daily respite from rigid distinctions between words and between self and other by allowing us to settle into the formless, the *wisdom beyond wisdom*—we chant in the Heart Sutra, the examination of formlessness chanted during many Buddhist ceremonies the world over. It is akin to dissolving the little wavelet of your individual personality back into the ocean to free it of all constraints.

Below the level of differentiation, meditation reminds the body viscerally of its relationship to all of it and that each named thing possesses an umbilical cord (easily discerned) connecting it to us. Sometimes efficiency demands that we use words and at other times seeing things, as it is requires that we *feel* the world beyond the confines of the word.

Most people assume meditation is a practice for the mind, but it may be even more important as a practice for the body. Daily, repetitive sitting strengthens our physical core and builds confidence in the inherent safety of zazen, instilling confidence and security into the body. This security permits our muscles to relax and release their stored freight of misconstrued ideas and trauma. Meditation offers us the deep release of seeing through every received mask, to recognize, in the words of the old Zen koan, *our original face before our parents met.* We can think of it as a refined technology for altering physical and mental awareness, and our access to its benefits is no further away than sitting down.

A PARABLE

The tomb was basically done when Buddy-Boy changed his mind—again! "Couldn't have a reed roof, could he? By God no," the Lone Ranger griped to himself, consumed by fury. "That'd never withstand the centuries, so now we spend our mornings finding the 'correct' trees and carving roof tiles. Couldn't do rectangles, oh no. They had to be like they were in Nepal!" The Lone Ranger had been running through similar monologues like this daily. His displeasure was obvious, but something was keeping him locked in orbit around the Buddha, and he was, by God, going to figure out what it was and free himself from this spell.

Why they had to be hand-made wooden roof tiles the Lone Ranger had no idea, but somehow, little insistent Buddy-Boy had found the right tree and knew how to make them. "Here we are, carving them until our hands bleed," the Lone Ranger complained to himself. A flat little rectangle would have worked just fine, but you couldn't argue with the guy; he would not budge.

That meant that for the past several weeks they'd been trekking to the high country to find local juniper—had to be dead *mind you, because Buddy-boy wouldn't kill a tick—which they split and shaved and polished, while Buddy-Boy fitted the viga rafters into perfectly shaped notches in the stone tops of the walls.*

He had to admit that the high country was worth the effort. The air was cool and clear. His body enjoyed working up a sweat climbing the hills and hauling back the slivered trees. He noticed that he had not been anxious or worried for weeks, and the discovery cheered him except for the one thing.

Three more months had gone by, and the Lone Ranger had become pretty irritated with their little dark-skinned friend, and he was spoiling for a showdown. The guy smiled all the time, no matter what you said. In response to questions or comments, he said "maybe" or "could be" and went back to what he was doing. The Lone Ranger wanted to strangle him.

That night, he washed with special care, pulled on his—he had to admit—impeccably cleaned and repaired white pants and shirt. (Where did this guy find the time? Didn't he sleep?) He buffed his boots and all the silver fittings on his holsters. He ate by himself— quail that Tonto had caught, a nettle soup he might have had in Paris, more of that good bread. He knew Tonto could tell he was pissed, but Tonto refused to catch his eye, or if he did, he looked right through him. Tonto spoke only once. "Have it your way," he said.

After dinner, the Lone Ranger dropped his plate into the bucket with soapy water made from some kind of onion-like, three-leafed root, walked purposefully over to the Buddha, and said, "Hey, Mister All-Is-One. I'm over here and you're over there, right?"

"As far as it goes," Buddha replied.

He reached over and knocked on the Buddha's knee with his fist. "You felt that, I didn't," the Ranger said with certainty.

The Buddha said, "Then how'd you know your hand didn't miss my knee?"

The Lone Ranger raised his hand and began a response, "I felt it in . . ." he caught himself from going further. "If I hit you, you feel it and I don't."

"Really?" the Buddha answered.

"I mean with a stick or something."

"I see," said the Buddha. "What's your point?"

"I'm me and you're you."

"Who said you weren't?"

"Well, you did. I mean, the all-is-one stuff."

The Buddha sighed. Boy, this guy was stubborn. "Did you ever have a sweetheart?"

"I had more than that," the Lone Ranger answered. "I had four wives."

"Okay," Buddha nodded. "What'd you call them?"

The Lone Ranger thought for a moment, and a pang like an electric shock coursed through him over the loss of Sally Allen. "Sometimes honey, sometimes sweetie. I dunno, sometimes just Sally or Clarita. Whatever."

"Same role, different names, right?" Buddha asked.

"Yes. So what?" the Lone Ranger asked.

"Well, if you look at the ocean on a choppy day, you can say wave or ocean, right? Both are true? It just depends which one you're concentrating on. That's like you and me, right? But then, there's the ocean or the all of it that we're both attached to and supported by."

The Lone Ranger said, "Well . . ."

Tonto sighed and said, ". . . not really separate."

The Lone Ranger sat still a long time.

The Buddha laughed and said, "What was your face before your parents met?" He flipped up into a handstand and rocked around the campfire on his hands. His robe, responding to gravity, fell over his upper body uncovering his butt so that it appeared that an ass and some man-junk was parading around the desert in a skirt, waving its arms. Tonto laughed so hard he was crying. The Lone Ranger made the crazy person sign, twirling his index finger near his ear. "I'm gonna report you to your master!" the Lone Ranger threatened.

"You do that!" the Buddha responded and disappeared.

By distracting his body and mind with the labors to build the treasure house, the Buddha has moved the Lone Ranger into a state of health and energy where he can begin to consider metaphysical inquiries. He's wrestling with the understanding of self and other, and the Buddha, without fighting, leads him gently along. Tonto seems to be getting it readily.

🜙 🜙 🜙

13
Seeing for the First Time

When I was in my early twenties, I was in love with a woman named Jesse Benton whose father was the American painter Thomas Hart Benton. I spent a part of each summer absolved of farm duties, living in Martha's Vineyard's wild "up-island" terrain near the Benton family compound. Tom was often accessible to the young people there, and his home was a gathering spot for a talented cadre of young folk musicians. He sometimes whipped out his harmonica to accompany the musicians congregating around Jesse, a mesmerizing singer of heart-aching soulfulness. One afternoon, I chatted with Tom while he worked on a particularly severe self-portrait. I inquired about the intensity of the expression on the face in his portrait. His reply was illuminating: "Painters are always trying to see things for the first time."

He continued to explain that the intensity of the self-portrait derived from his repeated looking away and then rapidly back into the mirror, intent on capturing a fresh view of himself.

I had a similar experience with another great visual artist, Roman Polanski, when I was performing in his film *Bitter Moon*. Whenever he had a decision to make about my costume or some prop I might carry, he would have me leave, change, and then return and "surprise" him. It was his way of ensuring that he was "seeing for the first time."

Thinking without language is akin to seeing again for the first time. All of us have perceived uncountable numbers of objects and experienced countless emotions during the course of our lives, and while we give lip service to the fact that no two instances are exactly alike, when our awareness attaches to something, almost before we know it, we have not only named it but also decided whether we like, dislike, or are neutral about it. Without thought, we have categorized it, compared it, and enmeshed it in a complex web of previously known concepts, events, values, memories, and predictions. Seeing things for the first time is another way of observing things as it is or being in the moment. Meditation is the practice of *just this,* day after day, year after year.

One of the towering giants of Buddhist practice and thought was a thirteenth-century priest named Dogen. After years of practice in Japan, first as a young Tendai monk and then as a Rinzai monk under Eisai, founder of Japanese Rinzai, from whom Dogen received transmission, Dogen was still not satisfied with his understanding and, at great personal risk, crossed the East China Sea and traveled to China, where he stayed for many years, eventually practicing with a teacher named Tiāntóng Rújìng, who taught a style of Chan Buddhism different from anyone else's. Dogen achieved liberation under this teacher and brought the radical, simplified practice stressing direct experience back to Japan, where he eventually founded the Eiheiji monastery, the monastic heart of Japanese Soto Zen.

One of his mysterious instructions to his students urged them to "think nonthinking."

I used to ponder that instruction ceaselessly, wondering what he could possibly mean. Images arise in the mind ceaselessly, and ending that process seemed impossible (and is not the point of meditating). Eventually, I discovered a distinction between *engaging* with one's thoughts—fascinated by them and ratcheted along by them, as if on a conveyor belt—and *observing* that mind stream dispassionately. Mind can be mind and the body can be the body without interference.

This is not *thinking* as we normally consider it. Thinking is being engaged with our thoughts, puzzling them out, responding to the feelings that arise, and liking or disliking what transpires in the mind. This is what Don Juan meant in the epigraph at the beginning of the book when he referred to *thinking while thinking.* Some Buddhist scholars translate Dogen's term as *not-thinking,* which feels off the mark to me. *Not*-thinking implies a command to not do something, and the implication is that it's within one's control—implying a self-effectuating action. The self in that phrase is extra and unnecessary. *Non*-thinking allows awareness to do what it will: monitor the flow without interference.

Observing yourself in a mirror while wearing a mask is also seeing for the first time. The novel face before you floods your brain receptors with so many new possibilities that the mind, seeking stability, assembles a new persona from the mask's clues. At rest, the mind is like the idling engine in a stick-shift automobile. With the clutch depressed the motor can idle, turning over with explosive force, yet no power is transmitted to the wheels until the clutch is released.

In meditation, the mind spins like that idling engine, according to its own self-organized principles, while the meditator observes, upright and unaffected, with his sequestered attention—the equivalent of the left foot depressing the car's clutch.

Thinking—*engaging* one's awareness with the train of thought—is like releasing the clutch, grasping the mental stream in the same way a clutch disk grips the engine's flywheel, harnessing its power, binding the mind's energy to the train of thought.

Observing the mind without undue engagement is a strategy to ensure the deepest possible intimacy with it. It supersedes limited, egoistic perspectives. It allows other beings, thoughts, and events to remain self-organized (which is what the word *wild* actually means) and to remain free from being warped by the intentions and judgments of others. This is never a stumble-free process, which is why Buddhists refer to mindfulness and meditation as a practice—a lifelong series of inevitable mistakes, fumbles, and corrections. Detachment does not mean not caring. Let's remember Quang Duc and his sacrifice; his passion and dedication to justice and liberty led him to place concerns for others even over his own life and suffering.

Thinking normally involves an act of will. The expression "I can't stop thinking about" something is actually stating "I don't know how to disengage from my thoughts." That's a good place to start because disengagement can be *practiced,* and various sects of Buddhism have developed many different exercises and methods to help people develop that practice.

The Tibetans, for instance, introduce new students to specific meditations designed to purify, calm, and concentrate the mind enough to take advantage of pure meditation—what the Tibetans refer to as *dzogchen.* Other sects preoccupy the mind with constant repetition of prayer or mantras or simply repeating the Buddha's name. All roads lead to Rome, but the one I am most qualified to discuss is Zen.

Zen practice begins by throwing students directly into the deep water of meditation with little preparation, burdening the attention with apparently minor concerns of posture, breath, and mudra and many formal, complex ceremonial procedures in the zendo. These concerns preoccupy students and prevent them from making 100 percent of their awareness available to the mind's talons.

A PARABLE

The Lone Ranger had been cheesed off the entire day, feeling that he'd been made a fool of the night before by petty trickery and word games. He did forty push-ups—twenty better than his last best—and washed and dressed meticulously, spoiling for an argument. As a precaution, he left his guns lying on his bedroll. He was that angry.

He stalked over to the Buddha, thrilled at the energy and vigor flowing through him after years of lassitude.

Tonto was scanning the horizon for Scout.

"You think I'm an ignorant dick-wad, don't you?" the Lone Ranger demanded, obviously upset.

The Buddha looked up sweetly. "What's a dick-wad?" he asked. "And why are you angry?"

"Don't be cute," the Lone Ranger said. "You think I have no inner life or something."

"I wonder about it sometimes, yes, because most of what you talk about are heroic deeds and 'stopping evil,'" the Buddha replied. "I don't know what that means. You do shoot people . . ."

"Only bad people," the Ranger interjected.

"Hmmm," Buddha replied. "Aren't good and evil Siamese twins?"

"A thief is bad," the Lone Ranger said.

"Suppose he's stealing to feed his family?" Buddha said.

The Lone Ranger was ready for that one. "The magnificence of the law is that it includes intention . . . but okay, a murderer then."

"I'm confused," Buddha said. "Don't you murder people?" When the Lone Ranger said nothing, Buddha continued, "Okay, what do you think about?"

"Well," he answered, relieved to be off the hook, "serious questions. For instance, do you think the universe is eternal?"

"Not really," the Buddha replied.

"Aha," said the Lone Ranger, squatting down eagerly before him as if preparing to wrestle. "So, therefore you must believe it's chronological."

"Not really," the Buddha replied.

"Well, do you think the universe is infinite?"

"Nope," said Buddha and munched some pine nuts Tonto had cleaned.

The Lone Ranger was not deterred. "Okay. Do you think that life is the same as the body?"

"Nope."

"Then you must think that life exists as 'other' than the body."

"Not me," said the Buddha.

"Do you believe we exist after we die?" The Lone Ranger folded his legs and was now sitting directly opposite the Buddha but experiencing some difficulty because his fashionable tight pants were restricting the blood flow in his legs and pinching his testicles.

The Buddha noticed this and folded his yellow robe to make a comfortable cushion. "Put this under your butt. It makes it easier to sit cross-legged."

The Lone Ranger did that. "Thanks," he said, "but you can't throw me off my game with kindness. Do you believe we exist after we die?"

"Oh," Buddha responded, "well, I'm not absolutely sure we exist before we die, but I guess, no."

"Okay, now we're getting somewhere. So, you've gotta believe that we don't exist after we die."

"Not me, buddy." The Buddha turned to Tonto with an outstretched palm for more pine nuts.

Growing frustrated, the Lone Ranger continued, "So that means you think we exist and don't exist after we die, right?"

"I didn't say that."

"Well, the only other logical option is that we neither exist nor don't exist after death."

"Good try," said Buddha, who was throwing pine nuts in the air and catching them in his open mouth with uncanny accuracy. The Lone Ranger didn't appear to notice because he was seriously pissed. "You have psychological problems, you know that? You need medication. You avoid every logical option I've offered."

"I'll answer you, but first, I can tell that your nuts are being strangled in those pants. Take 'em off, relax in your shorts, and we can chat."

The Lone Ranger whipped off his boots and pants and sat back down in his BVDs, elbows propped on his thighs, peering intensely at the Buddha, who spoke to him slowly and kindly.

"Look, Clayton, if I say the universe is eternal, it's my opinion. It's actually dozens of opinions really. If I say it's chronological, it's dozens of other opinions. Why talk about stuff that's beside the point? Opinions are beside the point. What is the nature of mind, of awareness? Those are questions whose answers can be experienced."

Indicating the Lone Ranger with his hand, he continued, "You *are relating the entire universe to something your ordinary mind can comprehend. It's so off the mark, but it's the same for most people. You ignore everything outside your own knowledge."*

"Well, who dies then or is 'reborn,' as you guys like to say?"

"Who lives?"

When the Lone Ranger appeared to be unable to reply, the Buddha continued, "To say reborn is off the mark. To say not reborn is not the point. To say neither reborn nor not reborn is not the point. You're trying to crack a walnut with a feather. What I teach is subtle, hard to get, and beyond logic, only available to lovers of wisdom."

"Oh man," the Ranger said. "You wear me out." Rising and starting off, he turned to the Buddha and said, "But I'm not done with you." He began hopping about on the hot sand and hobbled back over to pick up his boots and clothes. "This is why white people invented boots," he said snidely, casting a dubious glance at the Buddha's thin sandals.

"You look cute in those tighty whities," the Buddha answered, chuckling.

In the far distance, wild horses neighed and called. Tonto turned his head to listen. Scout was nowhere to be found.

The Lone Ranger has reached the limits of what is possible with words, logic, and syntax. He's about to be pushed beyond those capacities.

14
Buddha's Empty Hands

Peter was able to demonstrate how our perceptions of self get in the way of our ancient, instinctive knowledge about the character we are bringing to life. . . . Wearing a blank mask . . . reveals how we "wear" a mask every day, our own face, and what that unconsciously communicates to those we encounter. By considering [aligning with] what our mask communicates, we change all of our body language, and therein lies the key to freeing our infinite potential. A profound lesson for . . . everyday living.

MICHAEL STECHER, WORKSHOP PARTICIPANT

One of the qualities that first attracted me to Buddhist thought was understanding that, while all religions may encourage charity and kindness to strangers, their narratives usually require fealty to a particular savior or idea of God. Such insistence creates a perimeter separating those inside and outside the religion. Such borders inevitably exclude or devalue those who adhere to a different narrative.

Buddha's teachings are not necessarily involved with faith and narrative, and unlike all religions with which I have come in contact, they adhere more closely to objective and scientific truths. His teachings can be personally observed and verified. From this perspective, Buddhism is not precisely a religion. Buddha was a human being, not a miraculous or holy one. What he learned and deduced is available to any other human and does not demand fealty to his beliefs. Neither does it challenge the verities of other religions or scientific truth. Having said this, faith and worship appear to be two categories particularly dear to humans, and so there are sects of Buddhism that appear to be religions as we normally understand them. Zen, however, is not one of them.

Two thousand five hundred years ago a prince named Gautama once lived in a territory that is now part of Nepal. Legend states that his father, the king, went to great lengths to prevent Gautama from ever seeing human suffering. Despite his father's prohibitions, one day Gautama ordered his servant to take him outside the castle grounds, and he was confronted by the reality of old age, sickness, and death. He was so overwhelmed and shaken by the suffering he witnessed that he resolved to get to the root of it, and one night soon afterward he left the castle and his family and lived in the forest as an ascetic for six years.

Eventually, by concentrated effort and analysis, he pierced the delusions, confusions, and attachments of ordinary men and women and was liberated from all doubt and ignorance. He then dedicated himself to teaching what he had learned to others. This story has undoubtedly been amplified by legend over the twenty-five centuries since Gautama lived, but to Buddhist practice, the narrative is not all that important. Its point is only that he was so aggrieved by the suffering of the world that he resolved to understand and vanquish it. All claims of his practice can be verified by personal experience.

Primary among his intellectual contributions are the Buddha's clear expression of *dependent arising* and *emptiness*. By perceiving the entire world of form as irrefutably connected to everything else, he understood all nameable objects to be empty of any fixed, separate core of identity (self).

I am as composed of sunshine, water, oxygen, and microbes in the soil, which grew my food, as I am flesh and blood. The more deeply I investigate this, the more I can see that flesh and blood *are* the sunshine, water, oxygen, and so on—that these are invisible umbilical cords linking me to the entire universe. Since I have no separate existence without them, it is clear that "I"—in my conventional thinking of myself—do not exist as I once imagined.

Buddha observed clearly that every apparently single thing was dependent on multiple other things, which, in turn, were dependent on other things, creating what ancient Indian philosophers characterized as the Jewel Net of Indra. This likened the universe to a giant net with a faceted gem fastened at every intersection of the net's threads, each revealing and reflecting all the others. This metaphor of inclusion and mutual dependence disregarded nothing and excluded no one, not even ants and fleas.

Dependent arising includes thoughts, emotions, and impulses— which likewise depend on other conditions for their existence. On the surface it appears simple: an apple cannot exist without the apple tree and vice versa; the tree cannot exist without its leaves, and conversely the leaves cannot exist without sunlight, water, soil, bees, and so forth, therefore neither can the apple. The deeper implication is that because everything depends on other things for its existence, nothing possesses an independent, fixed core, which could be identified as the germ or essence of that nameable object, colloquially what we refer to as a self.

The Buddha never refuted our sense of self-awareness or the utility of a self. He never declared that the self did or did not exist. His understanding was that imagining self-awareness as fixed or permanent or reifying it as a fixed object corresponding to an organ is both unnecessary and false. It is false because we are claiming that we are a sole exception and asserting that a self (we can neither see, grasp, nor describe) exists without relationship to everything else, contravening the observable truth of universal mutual dependency.

There is no substance identifiable as "appleness" inside an apple. No matter how carefully one separates the peel, stem, fruit, or seeds or how microscopically one examines any of those parts, no germ of appleness can be discovered. Similarly, no germ of hand exists apart from the skin, muscle, ligaments, bones, blood, and nerves, and no self of personality exists independently of what Buddhist psychology refers to as *skandhas,* or "heaps," of form, feeling, impulse, sensation, and consciousness along with eyes, ears, nose, tongue, body, and mind, which constitute the collection of parts we call a human being.

Form includes material things, which can be sensed or felt. *Feelings* are physical or mental sensations that derive from our six sense organs— eyes, ears, nose, tongue, body, and mind contacting the objects of their attention. *Perceptions* include thoughts but also the knowledge that connects, compares, and associates things. *Mental formations* include volitional actions, attitudes, biases, and predilections—good, bad, or neutral. *Consciousness* is the awareness, the matrix everything floats in, but even consciousness is dependent upon the other skandhas and does not exist independently from them.

There are volumes about this egoless description of reality written in the *Abhidharma,* the Buddhist encyclopedia assembled in the third century after Buddha's death, to explain doctrinal issues raised by his teachings and to attempt to resolve disputes among various sects and factions that arose after Buddha died.[1] One can devote a lifetime to studying the nuances and implications of these various texts, but I am not as disposed toward scholarship (and neither is Zen) as much as I concentrate on the central point that the five skandhas are a *temporary* collection, the result of eons of human impulses and desires going all the way back to Lucy or Eve. They are conditioned by one another and the objects in the material world with which they are interrelated. In Buddhist psychology, there is no you independent of all of it. Suzuki-roshi sometimes said, in parsing a sentence like "I am walking," that "the I is extra."

*The liberating implication of Buddha's observation is that there is no discernible separate self within the component parts of our body—*eyes, ears, nose, tongue, and mind. What we refer to (and have reified as an object) as our self is *a concept,* a feeling, a cluster of awareness more akin to a cloud of vapor than a fixed entity. Suzuki-roshi points out that "all descriptions of reality are limited expressions of the world of emptiness."

This implies that our behaviors, attitudes, and habits and our self-limiting ideas—such as "well, that's how I am" or "I *always* do such and such"—are learned and are not built-in characteristics of a permanent physical entity. It means that our potential to change is not impeded by our physical form!

Search as we might, we will never find any physical equivalent for our self-awareness, what we call "me" and "I," because it is composed of nonself elements—which are in turn composed of other nonself elements. There is no identifiable us beyond our mutually supported awareness, and it is completely ungraspable, just like our ceaselessly rumbling train of thought.

Furthermore, there is no proof that awareness is singularly and solely ours and not, in some ways, shared by all sentient beings. When we gaze into the eyes of a dog or a hawk or a horse, we sense the awareness regarding us. That mutuality has helped us as a species to become experts in communicating with and understanding animal awareness and teaching them to do inconceivable things.

Near my home in Santa Rosa, California, a woman named Bonny Beguin (who invented the concept of service dogs) breeds and trains golden labradors and golden retrievers. Every dog she and her cohorts train learns *108* basic commands. Dogs that assist hemiplegic people or autistic people learn even more. These dogs can pick up dropped pill bottles, open refrigerator doors, and help disabled or injured people to dress and undress. They do it joyously without treats and bribery. Humans have trained dogs to find drugs and cadavers, pull wagons, carry food, and find lost men and women. Anyone who's ever ridden or witnessed a cutting horse separate a calf from the herd or watched sheepdogs respond to long-distance hand signals to round up sheep can confirm that they are observant animals who are fully aware of their task and often improvise the means to achieve their owner's desired result.

I live in a rural area where my dogs do not have to be leashed. When we walk about each morning and afternoon, I watch them dogtrot, stop to check the "doggie news" (scents left on blades of grass and bushes), and then suddenly stop and stare fixedly, having perceived something I cannot see or hear. They make me aware of how much more sensitive their hearing, sight, and smell is than my own. When they pick up an intoxicating scent, they make rapid detours to a source that may be twenty yards away, scampering in a dead run to that spot to investigate. All the while, they constantly check out where each other is and where I am. It is obvious that what I am watching is the play of their awareness and their problem-solving abilities, which are often so similar to human behavior.

The named objects we Westerners (like the Lone Ranger) believe to be absolutely real are, in Buddha's world, more like clouds of electrons assuming temporary coherence like the murmurations of birds. We have been instructed to recognize and label these temporary coherences, but once that is accomplished, efficiency leads us to unconsciously graft the permanence of the name onto what it is meant to represent, diminishing and often freezing out subtler levels of awareness.

Buddha's description of all things as empty is a logical conclusion of mutual dependence. This is why he describes the ceaseless, procreative energy of the universe as emptiness. The Heart Sutra, one of the core texts of Avalokiteshvara, the bodhisattva who embodies the compassion of Buddha, states clearly:

Form is not different from emptiness;
Emptiness is not different from form.
That which is form is emptiness;
That which is emptiness is form.

Discussing this, text Suzuki-roshi once explained this more fully.

We have to believe in something which has no form and no color—something which exists before all forms and colors appear. . . . No

matter what god or doctrine you believe in, if you become attached
to it, your belief will be based more or less on a self-centered idea.[2]

Why does he say "*have* to believe"? What is the imperative? His
implied meaning is that to reach a true and objective understanding of
"things as it is," we must drop self-centered perceptions and ideas.

In his book *Awakening the Mind: Lightening the Heart,* the Dalai
Lama goes so far as to define *ignorance* as "the belief that things exist
as they appear, independently and autonomously, without depending on
causes."

The "causes" for something's existence do not disappear once that
object or thought assumes form. They remain an underlying buttress,
visible or not. Mountain ranges are eventually worn to dust; bees live
several weeks to perform their duties and make their one teaspoon of
honey. Mayflies live twenty-four hours, humans sixty to a hundred
years, Joshua trees up to a millennium. As identified and named, they
appear to exist, sole and solitary, "without depending on causes," as the
Lone Ranger conceives of himself—but that is the *illusion* or *dream* to
which so many spiritual traditions refer.

15

The Devil You Don't Know

The Dalai Lama has reminded us that in the final analysis, the pursuit of wisdom and the practice of kindness does not require us to adopt a new religion . . . or any religion at all. There is nothing in Buddhism inherently contradictory to any religious practice. If you practice your own religion as a vehicle for kindness and empathy you could as well define yourself as a Jew-Budd, a Christ-Budd, or a Mus-Budd. Zen Buddhism is my path, and I have discovered utility and joy in its philosophy and practice. I can think of no necessary contradiction between Buddhist practice and the core beliefs of other practices, except for prejudices levied against nonbelievers, something all religions (and some rare Buddhist groups) are guilty of perpetuating.

Before humans viewed a photograph of Earth from outer space, it is understandable why one group of humans in a particular location could have considered themselves as "everybody" and believe that their expression of the sacred was universal. I was raised a secular Jew and so was attracted to that culture, which included reverence for learning and knowledge, wit, love of irony, nerve, and 5,700-odd years of survival wisdom. But I wasn't drawn to the religious services, which, to me as a child, appeared foreign and impenetrable. Also, these religious practices did not seem to guarantee that Jews would be markedly more evolved than others; their behavior was no better than what I observed among non-Jews. When I became older and convinced that my life required some spiritual ballast to stay upright, I was fortunate enough to discover Zen Buddhism. I remain attracted to it because of its tangible benefits and also because it professes (and usually practices) kindness to *all* others, including other species.

As a priest, I am called upon to perform ceremonies, most usually weddings and funerals, and counsel those who feel a need for it. Most of the marriages I've officiated have involved marrying people of different faiths whose own religions would not condone marriage to a nonbeliever. While the religion of either the bride or groom may have difficulty expressing generosity toward a member of another religion, Buddhism perceives the multiple forms of reality as masks of emptiness, and so a Buddhist priest can cheerfully step up to cement their bond. We joke that "Buddhists will marry anyone."

If we don't get too attached to our own standards of measure and favor our way above others, there are no problems in joining adherents of differing faiths and allowing them to develop practices together. It is in ordinary reality amid our everyday struggles with other humans and with ignorance, confusion, and doubt (not to mention the world's dramas, threats and dangers) that we humans are challenged to fashion an enlightened existence.

Compared with these challenges, living in a monastery is quite simple. Traditional Zen practice includes the understanding that after arduous monastic training, it is still necessary to season one's insights by practicing in the everyday, workaday world, usually for a longer period of time than one had practiced monastically.

Regardless of which school of Buddhism one might study—Japanese, Tibetan, Vietnamese, Korean, Cambodian, Thai, Indonesian, or Indian—it is often the case that many students, like myself, are drawn to it by the allure of enlightenment. Because enlightenment ("the wisdom that transcends likes and dislikes") has a name, it is easy to imagine it as a possession, a reified state, which can be identified, grasped, and attained. Many people misunderstand it in this way, despite the Buddha's assertion that enlightenment is our original nature.

The imagined magical promise of enlightenment may be a lure and a goad; it can foster dedication to our practice. But it may also lead us to excessively zealous practice modes, spiritual competitiveness, and self-centeredness. I know several old Zen students whose fervor was so intense that they now walk with canes because they ignored the suffering of their knees. Any practice may contain subtle traps for the unwary.

From the first day I read about Buddhism and enlightenment, I believed it to be a fence one catapulted over or burst through and, on the other side, emerged completely transformed—spontaneously cranking out wisdom, intuitive genius, and feats of psychic magic on demand. A more sober view could be read into this mysterious response of Suzuki-roshi to a student who asked him about enlightenment. "You might not like it."

He was indicating that the point at which the world you have always known falls away and awareness claims the territory once cordoned off by language and concepts, the entire universe appears as transitory as a soap bubble. There is no longer a single permanent thing to grasp or depend on. Personally, it was disorienting and unsettling to know, beyond a shadow of a doubt, that the Buddha himself and his teachings—which I had once established as a touchstone of certainty for decades—was, in the final analysis, as empty and ungraspable as everything else.

Even enlightenment cannot be depended on. In some ancient texts, such dependence is described as "sick monkeys . . . shackled in golden fetters." The golden fetters represent attachment, and the sick monkey remains attached to the dharma of Buddha. Fervent belief in Buddha and Buddhism can be delusionary unless it is revivified in tangible practice, moment after moment.

It ultimately became clear to me (as my teacher and others had warned) that even a peak experience is no final resting place for achievement.[1] There is always a further, higher peak to scale, and a new, more comprehensive vista to experience. Insight experiences like kensho are a clue that you're on the right track, but pride and self-satisfaction in one's personal achievement would be like continuing your journey with iron weights around your ankles. The great eighteenth-century Japanese Zen master Hakuin warned about such folly.

> Even though you once attain satori, it's best to regard it as insufficient, always insufficient. . . . If you yourself should break through into kensho, you must never remain satisfied with that small attainment. If you did, you would be committing a sin of such magnitude as to fill the vast heavens.[2]

So, now what? You might say, "Okay, everything is an expression of emptiness, without a kernel of self or permanence. Got it! What do I *do* with that knowledge? How does that help me?"

Even after experiencing emptiness of body, speech, and mind and understanding that attaching to any state will only create new problems, Hakuin described this state as "a dead man peering goggle-eyed from a coffin." (Without the discipline and courage to behave as if the masks of the world are real, despite knowing better [what Don Juan refers to as "controlled folly"], there is a danger of sinking into despair or the anarchic belief that nothing means anything.)

Unless your life is orderly and disciplined and your intention fixed on compassion, without such ballast, you become a leaf scattered before the wind, still blown about by fear and desire and tossed between endless temptations, fleeing dread and surrendering to hypnotic attractions. This is the failing of Rimbaud's model of seeking wisdom by attempting to destroy the self and its limits. Such errors snatched Kurt Cobain; killed my pal Janis Joplin, my brothers Emmett Grogan, Sweet William, and Duvall Lewis; and very nearly got me. In discussing Rimbaud's self-destructiveness with me, Gary Snyder observed that "in Rimbaud's time, the middle and upper classes were so fixated on rationalism that there was no space in the society for wild minds and imaginative freedom. But today, the middle and upper classes are indulgent to the point of suicide, and it is now the critical responsibility of the artist to model health, wisdom, and a good life."

This is an important caution. If we begin meditation as a search for enlightenment, imagining an "I" over here and enlightenment somewhere else, an exotic state somewhere to be attained, we create an artificial distinction and reinforce their separation even while attempting to unite them. It's like dangling a carrot in front of a donkey to keep it moving forward.

Trying to *attain* enlightenment is ignoring the Buddha's admonition that our natural state is already enlightened, but our attachment to passions, delusions, and anger (Hakuin's "nails and wedges") that obscures our knowledge of it. Spiritual practice is the way to clear away the brambles of desires, delusion, and selfishness to express what is already luminous within us. Having said that, it's also true that the concentrated meditative effort to solve in an important question often brings one to the point where the ego may surrender for a while and allow perception of things as it is. That is no resting place or final destination; it is a source to remember. When we see little snatches of the moon fragmented through tree branches or partially obscured by a cloud, we *sense* the whole moon. In that same way any letter from emptiness—the sound of a cricket or the bark of a crow—can remind us of the whole thing.

Hakuin's final decisive enlightenment occurred in his forties after numerous previous satoris. His deep realization was that the Buddha's Eightfold Path *itself* (which includes error and effort) *is* enlightenment and that a bodhisattva's mission must be practicing that path, with or without and before and after enlightenment, until all beings are saved. As an antidote to spiritual competition, bodhisattvas declare that they will be the last to be enlightened, accepting it only after they have first helped all other sentient beings across the divide.

That understanding became the organizing principle of the rest of his life. Until that night, according to his own writing, Hakuin's practice had been overly directed toward his own personal awakening.

From that point on, however, his efforts, through whatever means—cartoons, art, lectures, teaching—reflected his deep understanding that one may not even have a peak experience (kensho or satori), but trying too hard to achieve it, at the expense of dedicating oneself to the Eightfold Path at the expense of considering the needs of others, is a serious error. *The evidence of enlightenment is the life it expresses.* My teacher Chikudo Lew Richmond once cautioned me that "if you are not kind and helpful to others, who cares what your personal spiritual experiences have been?"

Buddhism could be defined as the practice of living by focusing on just this moment, never knowing the next moment, and going forward in this way, breath by breath, moment by moment, trusting that we possess everything we need to make our way. In such a state, everything one meets is Zen. It is not a mental event or a state of mind that can be retained or "figured out."

A kensho experience may be only a few vivid moments, but even an inch of travel is significant if you turn a corner. Afterward, one returns to ordinary life with its welter of confusions and problems, but this does not mean that nothing will have changed. As with glimpses of the moon, small daily events will remind us of enlightenment and keep us on course.

Life is like this, as well, when we surrender even temporarily to a mask. We do not know precisely how or why revelations pour through us, but we act fearlessly, with a certainty and flair that often eludes us in our everyday life. We do not know how penicillin works either, but we've learned to trust its efficacy. Tasks performed with a mask's power have a spontaneity and courage we can't exactly control but which we can ride in the same way a skilled kayaker rides a river—not controlling the energy but using it playfully. In such moment, we don't ask ourselves, "How do I look?" or "How am I doing?" There's no time to become an "objective" observer of our own existence and remain in that moment. Life is on full go all the time. I love the old joke of a fellow who leaped off the top of the Empire State Building and while falling past the fortieth floor was overheard muttering, "So far, so good!" In just that moment, he was correct.

A PARABLE

It was late at night, and the Buddha and Tonto were sitting cross-legged, knee to knee, conversing quietly. Silver was asleep and the Lone Ranger as well, lying with his head resting against his horse's shimmering neck, his arms crossed. Crickets and desert frogs chirped and croaked, and the sky glimmered with chips of light. Tonto was staring into the sand, tracing circles with his finger, speaking softly.

"I don't understand this world, Buddha. It's been good to me, really; I can't complain. It's brought me a nice house, a good wife and kids, plenty of money, and my thoroughbreds, but in the old days, being an Indian meant something. The world made sense. We believe that a woman gave birth to twins—one was named Teharonhiawako, or Holder of the Heavens. He was the good twin. His brother, Sawiskera, or Mischievous One, was the evil twin. We had to choose who we'd follow. We tried to behave right. We had shamans who understood the mysteries to help us. We respected other creatures; we didn't take more than we could use, you know? We cherished life. We prayed. But look how it all turned out. I mean, really . . . I . . ."

"It's hard to see one's culture and lands disappear," the Buddha responded kindly. "My father's kingdom was invaded, and my people killed, and it generated so much sorrow in me and continued to revisit me for many years. Enlightenment does not protect us from that. I'm human, so are you. We will never escape that in this lifetime. But I teach karma, consequences. A small act over time may generate large consequences. This is the world we have, the only one we have. We must learn to live in it and find peace and meaning as it is! Perhaps I can help you."

The Buddha hopped up as if he were weightless. He adjusted

Tonto's hands in his lap. "Lay the back of your left hand on the palm of the right. Touch the tips of your thumbs together lightly to make a nice fat circle. That's your attention gauge. If your thumbs come apart or the circle collapses, you know you've stopped paying attention.

"Now sit up as if a string was pulling the top of your head into the sky. Tuck your chin just enough to feel the back of your neck growing a little longer. Let your stomach pooch out, and keep your eyes open, gazing down about four feet ahead of you. That's it!

"For the first couple of minutes count your exhales—first one is 'one,' second's 'two,' up to ten. Extend the count for the length of the exhale, softly, like you're taking good care of each breath you release into the world. Then start over. When you lose count, just begin again. Don't criticize yourself. After a while, you can drop the counting and just maintain an awareness of your breathing while keeping your posture erect and your thumbs in good order. That's it. Let your thoughts do what they want to. This is your real life right now. Everything else is a memory or a guess of what's coming. You'll get it."

The Buddha walked away softly, disappearing into the gathering dark as if he'd been absorbed by it. He turned once to see Tonto sitting erect, looking inward. He was still there the next morning. That night, just before he turned in, the Buddha set a bowl of fresh water in front of him. Tonto didn't notice.

The next morning Tonto was gone.

Tonto gets down to core human issues. Buddha can't solve them; Tonto must. Some trust has been established by watching the Buddha for all these months, some appreciation for his calmness and lack of self-importance has led Tonto to make this confession to him. The Buddha has taught him how to meditate.

⑀ ⑀ ⑀

16
Even Buddha
Can Betray You

It must be admitted that there are some shadowy implications to emptiness that must be acknowledged, tricky currents and winds that can lead us off a good course and onto dangerous rocks. Emptiness is not personal. It is a fact, like lightning. Because everything is made up of other things, they remain empty of a self. This profoundly impersonal dynamic generates and absorbs civilizations, mountain ranges and stars, individuals and amoebas as rapidly as it generates them. One could say that the world operates with an impersonal coldness in which—rendered equal by death—our personal wishes and dreams count for no more than dust in the road. The fact that all things are empty of self renders us radically equal of all other transitory expressions.

This can be an unnerving proposition to accept. It is not easy for me to accept myself as composed of the same stuff as Hitler or Pol Pot or, perhaps, President Trump and with an ability to harm others equal to theirs. I would prefer to consider myself associated only with great and good men and women in a lineage of heroes, but this is a mental pet. In reality it is a reductive impulse, like trying to pour a gallon of water into a half-pint jar. The gallon is "all of it"—reality—the half-pint jar is my small mind picking and choosing what it likes and dislikes, shrinking the world to a comfortable, manageable size. We can get away like this in most instances for a long time, but eventually reality triumphs.

The danger is that superficial understanding of this radical equality could be used to justify heartless, sociopathic behavior. If everything is empty, one might be lulled into believing that nothing matters. If everything is equal, why *not* take a life, lie, cheat, or steal if you feel like it? What's the crime in bursting a soap bubble? Why not exploit or oppress others for your own benefit, raze the landscape, and kill endangered species if it's all empty?

Counteracting such shallow thinking is why all religions strive to constrain their transcendental impulses within tight frames of morality and ethics. Without considering the other's life equally important as our own (because it *is* our own), superficial understanding can be as destructive as egoism.

At one point in his sorcerer's explanation, Don Juan instructs Carlos Castaneda about how stopping the world (kensho in Buddhist terms) requires an unbending will. He labels the ability to act in a world leveled by death as "controlled folly," moderating one's actions *as if* they were important, despite knowing that they are not. Don Juan instructs him.

> A man of knowledge chooses any act and acts it out *as if* [emphasis mine] it matters to him. His controlled folly makes him say that what he does matters and makes him act as if it did, and yet he knows that it doesn't; so, when he fulfills his acts, he retreats in peace.[1]

In Don Juan's shamanism, the universe is ruled by power not kindness nor compassion. His world is that of a Yaqui Indian, and that reality was perceived as one of contending powers. Even so, the detachment of controlled folly allows all other entities and beings the full freedom to be what they are. Don Juan's insight is personal; Buddha's is collective, and his collective represents *all* sentient beings.

The Buddha's reply to Don Juan might be the addendum that deep understanding leads us directly to compassion, produced by the knowledge that each expression of form is a precious, unrepeatable event, passing away before us. That form can be short-circuited and undercut by selfish intention and greed, which is why Don Juan cautions Carlos sternly to follow a path with a heart. A student once asked Suzuki-roshi about power. His response of "don't use it" was more than a caution against employing shortcuts or force but also an echo of the paramount importance of fixing one's intention on compassion or Don Juan's path with a heart.

The Buddha goes to great lengths to spell out his Eightfold Path and Four Noble Truths, grounded in his profound insight that the entire universe is one interdependent single entity Participating wisely requires consideration of the other—and implies striving for agreement and having the elasticity to compromise if life is to continue. This is as true for the plants Don Juan apologizes to before he picks them as it is for humans and the animals we eat.

Both Don Juan's and Buddha's descriptions are based on this radical equality and the deep knowledge that, beneath our personal confusion, *intuitions* offer us reliable guidance for surviving and achieving a harmonious life with the world as it is.

If you have something better to do than work on yourself, you should do it, but I have yet to see even the most monumental works of man immune to destruction by the shadows of egoism, greed, and envy. I hope that I have piqued your curiosity enough to inspire your giving Buddhist thought and meditation a fair try.

Like Don Juan's steely dedication to a path with a heart, followers of the Buddha train their attention to dwell unbendingly on kindness and compassion. The other option is the world of cruelty, violence, strife, and destruction, fanned before our attention by the daily news.

It is particularly painful to me to be aware that recently Buddhists in Myanmar were persecuting, torturing, and killing members of a Muslim peasant minority called the Rohingya, perverting the essence of the Buddha's teaching. The best use I can make of that knowledge is to remind myself how easy it is for *any* of us to stray from mindfulness and compassion. Perhaps it was his memory of serving as a priest in Manchuria constantly doing memorials for the Japanese civilian population. So many wanted services that he'd walk down the street chanting to cover the houses en masse. Usually the demand was so great there was no time to enter homes. People would run out and make offerings. Perhaps that experience caused Suzuki-roshi to stress: "No matter what god or doctrine you believe in, if you become attached to it, you[r] belief will be based more or less on a self-centered idea. This idea is more important and of longer duration than Buddhism itself."

A PARABLE

The Lone Ranger woke early, climbed out of his bedroll, and stood pissing, gazing at the striated red-ocher cliffs and rubbing his belly contentedly. It was relaxing here, being in one place—none of the old pressure and anxiety concerning the silver mine or arguing with Tonto's bullshit about "white genocide."

"Geez, Louise. We're an odd friendship," he mused.

He looked over to where Silver lay stretched out asleep, expecting to see Tonto, but he was not visible. "Maybe he went looking for Scout," he thought, though his absence was a tad startling. He couldn't remember the last time they'd been out of one another's sight. He did a slow 360 degrees, pissing a circle around himself in the sand, feeling like a little kid, but found Tonto nowhere in his field of vision. He walked over to the Buddha, who was meditating. He waited awhile to be noticed and, when that failed, returned to his gear and dressed himself. By the time he returned, the Buddha was building a small fire.

"Where's Tonto?" he inquired.

"Gone," said the Buddha, blowing gently into last night's embers.

Puzzled, the Lone Ranger inquired, "Gone? Where?"

"Gone beyond," the Buddha replied, rising.

"Beyond where?" the Lone Ranger demanded with some heat and perhaps a hint of panic.

"Beyond beyond," the Buddha answered, indicating that the Lone Ranger should follow him. They walked a few yards off the sand onto a small hardpan flat. A perfect circle about three feet in diameter had been scribed in it with a stick. Just outside the perimeter of the circle was a smaller circle—surrounding Tonto's leather headband and the single eagle feather he always wore.

Pointing to it, the Lone Ranger said, "What's that mean?"

"He's given himself up."

"That's crazy!" the Lone Ranger said. "Given himself up? To whom?"

"Just the idea of himself," the Buddha replied.

"When's he coming back?"

"I don't think he is," the Buddha said.

"Well, he's left Scout. Jay would never do that. He wouldn't leave without saying goodbye! We're friends, for Chrissakes," he insisted, his voice rising in pitch uncontrollably.

"He's not Jay anymore," the Buddha said. "Or Tonto, either. Look, his footprints are heading east, toward Mohawk country."

The Ranger appeared agitated, whirling his hands as he spoke. "That's crazy. He's my faithful sidekick! He's my best friend. Shit, he's my only friend."

Seeing the Lone Ranger's distress, Buddha added, in a kindly tone, "Maybe it's time to be your own best friend. Move your camp over next to mine if you want."

"How'm I gonna take care of two horses?" the Ranger demanded querulously.

"There's only one horse here," Buddha observed.

The Lone Ranger was agitated. "Hey, we've been together thirty-five years. He can't . . . I mean . . . He just left?! We've never been separated, really. Christ!"

The Buddha regarded him with compassion and said softly, "Happens to all of us."

The next day the Lone Ranger remained agitated. Silver was restless, pacing nervously and whinnying for Scout, abrading the Lone Ranger's nerves. Small dust devils of wind peppered his skin with sand. He had no one to talk to while Buddha meditated, and he became increasingly restless.

Buddha continued what he'd announced at breakfast as his "day of meditation." Sometime in the late afternoon, while he sat, comfortably sheltered by a magnificent cottonwood tree, the Lone Ranger's two boots entered his field of vision and remained there, unmoving.

At first, Buddha perceived them as twin alligators, which soon morphed into little Negro babies clutching the tree trunks of the Lone Ranger's calves and then reformed themselves into tiny submarines emerging from the sand. The Buddha's eyes cleared, and he looked up to discover the entirety of the Lone Ranger standing before him, hands on hips, staring down at him intently.

"You want me to take my mask off, don't you?" he said.

"Why not?" Buddha responded.

"I'm the only person whose star on the Hollywood Walk of Fame has my name and the name of my character. Do you know why?"

"Nope."

"Because people love the Lone Ranger. He was the original 'good guy' in a white hat. Yes, he shot some people, but he shot them selectively and only bad guys, not like today's machine-gun butchers. He helped the poor and widows and orphans. Being the Lone Ranger made me a better person. That didn't happen when I played Zorro, and I wore a mask there too. Once I got the Lone Ranger role, I didn't want any other. I'll continue wearing the white hat and black mask until I ride up into the big ranch in the sky. I'm proud of that decision."

The Buddha regarded him in a kindly manner. "You do realize that you died in Los Angeles in 1999, on December 28, right?"

"What the hell does that have to do with it?" the Lone Ranger answered petulantly. "Jay died, too, and you didn't give him any

horseshit. The horses died, too, but obviously they're still here. Everything's still here, somewhere."

"Well, what I'm getting at is where is 'the big ranch in the sky,' pal? You're out in the middle of the New Mexican desert, and you're still haunted by figments of your own mind. Can't you get over disappointing your dad by not becoming a doctor? He was proud of you, your success and all, you know. You could relax a little. Retire some of your old ideas?"

The Buddha mimicked the Lone Ranger's voice with startling perfection: "I just don't feel alive without takin' risks . . . I don't care about bein' happy. My job is to do good on Earth and inspire people. Silver and I are on ads for Silvercup Bread. It's not my fault if it's all bleached white flour and lard . . . goddamn hippies and their whole-grain bullshit. It was good enough for me and my kids. My face is on a 44-cent stamp, did you know that? My face is the face of God on Kent Twitchell's mural on the Otis Parson Institute in LA . . ."

The Buddha stopped because the Lone Ranger was trembling, regarding him with horror. His eyes were opened wide and his jaw sawed up and down, while he licked his lips like a nervous dog. "How did you?" he began and then stopped. "Who the hell are you?" he asked. "You're not a servant at all, are you?"

"Oh, come on, Jack," the Buddha answered, "that's just a cheap trick with time and space."

"You knew my real name was Jack?"

"Yeah, it's on the internet."

"Holy shit." The Lone Ranger sat down hard, facing the Buddha, lost in thought. After a while he said, "You know my thoughts. That's scary." He sat bolt upright, "You don't have a master, do you?"

The Buddha winked and held a raised finger to his lips and said, "You got me there. No, I have no master. I'm just your own innate wisdom, pal, in convenient gift wrapping."

"Oh God, no, don't!" The Lone Ranger grew pale and started to sweat. He looked around to make sure no one was observing them and

then he leaned in close and whispered, "So were you lying about the reward?"

"I didn't lie about anything. I just said what I had to take you out of your head and into your body. To make you strong again. You did the rest."

"What about the gold coin?"

The Buddha pulled the gold coin out of his hem. He peeled off the gold foil wrapping and handed the Lone Ranger the chocolate interior. "I never said it was gold. Your greed made it gold, just like your fear makes you think that you're hiding something from me. You're stuck, buddy. Poor Jack Moore is a hungry ghost trapped in the Lone Ranger's clothes. No peace there, cowboy. Of course, Jack Moore's a mask, too, but you haven't caught on to that yet."

The Lone Ranger said, "I think I'm gonna be sick."

The Buddha handed him a bowl of tea and said, "This'll settle your stomach."

Silver whinnied.

The Lone Ranger addressed Silver with tears in his eyes. "You miss your old buddy, don't you, pal?" and then he began sobbing like a little boy.

The Lone Ranger has finally exposed his narrative, exposed his attachment to his reputation and who he is, and is now beginning to see things as it is. By realizing that the Buddha is not a servant and by getting a taste of his power, his reality is scrambled, and he surrenders to confusion and loss.

17

Locating and Listening to Your True Self

Once, during a long international plane flight, I struck up a conversation with a Polish gentleman in the next seat and learned that he had once been Albert Einstein's personal secretary. He told me a story about Einstein during the time he was editing his manuscript, which would introduce the unified field theory* to his peers. Einstein was seated editing before a sunny window one day, when a beetle flew in and landed on the manuscript. Einstein became mesmerized by it and afterward withheld the publication of the unified field theory for nearly two years, confessing to his secretary that he had no idea how that beetle had come to be, what its life was about, and what his own relationship to it might be. In the light of such ignorance, he felt presumptuous reducing the entire universe to a formula.

This story is a clear example of humility and restraint, and both are difficult and subtle practices. It's obvious to most of us how suppressing

---

*The fundamental forces (or fundamental interactions) of physics are the ways that individual particles interact with each other. According to this theory (at least my understanding of it), every interaction observed in the universe can be broken down to generally four types of interactions: gravity, electromagnetism, weak interaction (or weak nuclear force), and strong interaction (or strong nuclear force). Scientists suspect that they may be emanations from a common, underlying field and have, for many years, sought proof of that unified field theory.

hatred, rage, and violent impulses are beneficial and how inappropriate sexual behavior and dishonesty are harmful to others. There are other actions we may commit, however, where the violence is so cloaked or disguised that we may not even recognize it. It may appear to be benign but still harm others.

Restraining ourselves in these areas is difficult because we tend to underestimate the toll that emotional states like irritation and impatience, sarcasm, and demeaning and shaming language can wreak on others. We may even disguise them to ourselves as *instructive* for the party they're directed toward.

In a recent book about secular ethics, His Holiness the Dalai Lama gave the example of a river polluted by an industry—say a mining refinery or an industrial plant.[1] He pointed out that *every user* of that industry's product is complicit in that industry's pollution. He uses this example to point out that, in an interdependent world, we can harm others without intending to or realizing that we are and to urge us to heighten our sensitivity, discernment, and conscientiousness and our humility. In much the same way, many Caucasian people are now learning how the systems of justice and finance in the United States cause pain and death to African Americans. Often believing that because they are never rude to a black individual that they cannot be racist, they allow themselves to sidestep responsibility for the system under which they profit while their black neighbors suffer.

Restraint helps us in determining how much of anything we really need, which in turn contributes to how much of the Earth we consent to transform into a commodity. Do we really need garden gnomes and fake stones for gardens? Little vacuums to suck up spiders?

We all love our computers and consider them nonpolluting wonders, but are they really? What do we actually know about the environmental costs of mining silicon and the rare metals required to make them? What is their relationship to the wars being fought elsewhere to control those raw materials? Many of the developed world's outmoded computers are sent to China where impoverished people strip and burn them for copper and other recyclables, suffering extreme health damage as a result. Why is it not the responsibility of industry to collect the harmful products it produces and mitigate the environmental damage of their disposal?

The Dalai Lama does not write to make us feel bad but to expand awareness of our actual reality, our interconnections with others and the planet, and to highlight our personal responsibility as citizens, consumers, and inhabitants of Earth. At the very least, his perspective makes most local political deliberations appear to be as simplified as the illustrations in coloring books for children.

Internal housekeeping—cleaning out the cobwebs of old habits—is like dusting and straightening up our household interior. If we persevere with meditation, our minds become tender and receptive enough to drop (or at least soften) language, concepts, and fixed ideas. At such moments, the world stands before us revealed in its suchness, as it always has been, unmediated by concepts and judgments, beyond form and emptiness, beyond the limits of grammar and syntax. But it is not necessary to experience such a heightened moment to live an enlightened, compassionate life.

Even without such an awakening, attentiveness will always pay its own freight in terms of deeper intimacy and appreciation of self and other. When we fully appreciate that ideas of self are extra, that we are as empty of self as a soap bubble, *bodhicitta* (pronounced bodey-cheetah)—an ancient Sanskrit word (बोधिचित्त) indicating the compassionate impulse to save all beings from their delusions and suffering—arises within us spontaneously. It is no longer possible to distinguish oneself as quite so separate from the rest of it, increasing our appreciation of the miraculous aspect of every single existence in the universe.

INTELLIGENCE AND INTUITION

When we believe that our intelligence can solve all problems, we do so at our peril. Everything has a shadow, unseen dimensions and interconnections that may cause unintended consequences. The truth is intelligence has no *moral* valence. It is not a compass whose needle reliably selects positive, ethical outcomes. Believing that it does is a dangerous delusion that ignores a host of hidden consequences.

Intelligence can, with equal facility, design a hospital or a concentration camp, invent a life-saving vaccine, or fashion a toxic nerve gas. It can organize speech to inspire compassion and collaboration or it can be used to foment hatred and division. It is as useful to a despotic warlord as it is to a loving mother. Failure to account for the shadows of intelligence has created many of humankind's most horrific catastrophes from Hiroshima to the Holocaust, from the genocide in Rwanda to the murderous wars in Syria and Yemen and the current mass extinctions of entire species, occurring as I write. To this grim list, we must also add our planet's currently imperiled state threatened by stockpiles of nuclear weapons locked and loaded in fire-on-warning alert.

Part of the shadow is due to the reductive, discriminating quality of intelligence, its logical "if this, then that" deductive approach to isolated problems. But too often, emotional states like fear or greed are not factored into what appear to be mechanical formulas to achieve some goal. By removing a dilemma from its full context, a solution for one part of the problem may become the destruction of another.

The alternative is considering the wholistic world of mutual dependence—Buddha's explanation of dependent origination. The shadow of this interdependent wholistic world is that it is too vast and byzantine to be puzzled out by intelligence. Too much data floods human receptors at any given instant to make logical decisions always possible. In an interdependent universe, a reductive process like intelligence or logic will never be inclusive enough or as effective as mental processes that sample larger areas of the brain for pattern, connection, memory, and coherence. Consequently, in the world of interdependence, *intuition* is usually a more apt and effective guide.

Intuition is an older, more mysterious ability than intelligence and shared by many primates. Composed of *intelligence, memory,* and *emotion,* intuition activates larger areas of the brain than intelligence alone. It also operates more rapidly, classifying numerous impressions and data units into decision-oriented impulses. Through intuition, humans have learned to rapidly distinguish real danger from anxiety, discriminate friends from foes, and develop remarkable works of art and science. Sometimes, when prompted by extreme stakes, intuition delivers startling, counterintuitive solutions for survival. When lightning struck the south side of Mann Gulch at the Gates of the Mountains, a canyon over five miles (8 km) long that cuts through a series of 1,200 foot ridges, it burned so hot and so fast that thirteen firefighters were killed when they could not flee the flames. Three survived, two by luck, and the third, the foreman Wagner "Wag" Dodge, by lighting a fire at his own feet and burning a clear hole into which he stepped . . . and lived.

Lest we succumb to the comfort that this wholistic view is, by itself, a panacea for the shadows of intelligence, this perspective also casts its own shadow. Human history is replete with disastrous examples of grand schemes (often categorized as "the big picture") that sacrificed lives, cultures, species, and environments to human delusion and blind faith. Allegiance to delusional plans can spell doom to any imagined success. After all, one might demand: What is a butterfly, frog, or salamander habitat compared with the potential benefits of a hospital? What is a wetland in the face of housing shortages for humans? It may appear logical to make such sacrifices in pursuit of anthropocentric goals and ideologies, but the tens of millions of human deaths attributed to Hitler, Mao Tse-tung, and Stalin and the murder of a million Tutsi by Hutus in a hundred days should (but rarely does) give all "heroic" thinkers cautionary pause. Closer to our everyday experience, how many times have you driven by dead animals on the road, killed because the road separated these wild creatures from water, food, and critical habitat? The cost of adding tunnels under the roadbeds would have been minimal during construction, but it is doubtful that anyone even considered the needs of the animal realms who share the planet with us.

Americans are self-congratulatory about our generosity and many contributions to the world and our privileged life. We consider ourselves exceptional, but our privileges, wealth, and luck do not exempt us from the consequences of poor behavior. Protecting our wealth has led us to create military and intelligence budgets as large as the next nine largest military budgets of other nations, starving schools, medical care, affordable housing, childcare, and reasonable salaries for nurses, teachers, restaurant workers, waiters, and those who care for our aged.

Blind self-assurance and pursuit of wealth led directly to the ethnic cleansing of Native Americans and a four-century reliance on chattel enslavement and Jim Crow laws to subjugate and deprive African Americans of equal rights, creating, as a by-product, much of the economic inequality, instability, and rancor fretting us today. To that crime we need to add the oppression of millions of immigrants and poor indentured servants who remained indebted to overlords who brought them to America. The consequences of these enduring problems should remind us of the dangers of uninvestigated beliefs. There are no perfect humans nor any who have not made egregious mistakes. We might excuse Thomas Jefferson's ownership of slaves because he was a man of his times, when slave owning was still acceptable, but can we excuse a man who would free his half-black children but not the African mother who bore them? The first step toward repairing the consequences of any error is seeing it clearly, acknowledging it, and apologizing to those we have harmed. We can be grateful to Jefferson and Washington and other slavers for the gifts they've bestowed upon us, but we should not use their good deeds to camouflage the truth.

The extinction of the passenger pigeon, the massacre of 500 million native buffalo, and the mass extinctions of birds, frogs, salamanders, elephants, rhinoceros, jungle gorillas, leopards, jaguars, bears, and other species currently underway are a direct consequence of blindness to the unique value of each individual expression of the universe and the role it plays contributing to the whole. Sacrificing them to the big picture, overmuch reliance on the wholistic, creates consequences—such as the death of 50 percent of all coral reefs over the past fifty years because intelligence (and greed) have privileged the production of riches for humans over the limitations we would have to endure to ensure their continued existence.

From a Buddhist perspective, each and every one of the "ten thousand things" is a miraculous expression of the common, creative energy of the universe, expressed with equal standing to all other things and possessing its own inherent right to existence by having been expressed by creation. One housefly may not mean much to a human, but as a species, houseflies would not exist without meaning something to the universe.

These two perspectives may appear to exclude one another, but they more closely resemble the relationship between a wave and the ocean or that of water to ice and steam—different manifestations of a common source. Any conclusion deduced from either perspective alone, no matter how sensible or logical it may appear at first look, *is at best only half right,* which is also to insist that all one-sided conclusions are half wrong. No ideological system or worldview highlights its own shadows for us. That is the province of wisdom, and that is the terrain we seek when we allow the ego its holidays and plug our spinal telephones into the main trunk line of creation—the nature of mind.

Our insistence on personal liberty (without ever defining what we mean) or considering deeply what liberty might actually bode for others in an interdependent universe is comparable to our certainty about political theories and ideologies, our religious beliefs, and our economic theories. No matter how appealing they are, they are also, *at best,* only partially correct because they exclude from consideration alternative, equally valid descriptions of reality. Without including those failures in our plans and dreams, we cannot strategize to nullify the implications of their shadows. This is why we so often remain helpless before the onslaught of unintended consequences, which perpetually fret our hopes.

An ancient Buddhist epigram expresses this situation perfectly.

A clay Buddha cannot cross water.

An iron Buddha cannot pass through a furnace.

A wooden Buddha cannot pass through fire.

The epigram reminds us that no fixed idea works in every circumstance. Clinging to favored narratives and beliefs, while excluding all others, forces us to accept unworkable solutions that may appear functional and clever because they satisfy ideological or political problems, but they will ultimately fail to resolve the problems they've been advanced to solve and will always generate unintended consequences, which will catch us off guard.

The Japanese have a perfect image for such thinking. It is called *tamban-kan* and translates as "one board fellow." It denotes a man carrying a wide board on its edge across his shoulder. The man can see everything on one side of the board, but the board blocks the view of everything on the other side. Rigid adherence to ideas, ideologies, or philosophies—whether liberal, conservative, Democratic, Republican, evangelical, socialist, or even Buddhist—is like being tamban-kan because while the ideas usually remain rigid, the universe itself is in flux. Perhaps this is why Suzuki-roshi's book *Not Always So* was initially unnamed.

Masks allow us to peek around the corners of identity and plug into our spinal telephone whose receiver is plugged directly into the universe. When we do this, we meld concepts and ideas, mix things up and regard them from improbable positions, and by doing this receive startling and unexpected insights.

In a lecture once, Suzuki-roshi observed that the Japanese prepare all the ingredients of their meals separately: rice, soup, pickles, and so forth. When they exist separately, they do not nourish us; it is only when they are all mixed together in the stomach that we receive their benefits. Like masks, meditation returns us to the mix of everything, beyond our ideas, concepts, and philosophical positions, and by surrendering to this formless ocean, we are nourished in our individual existences.

The collective inheritance of consciousness of our species includes spiritual adepts (from every culture) who have mastered the simultaneous perception of both worldviews—the singular and the interdependent—to achieve a level of understanding deeper than either affords singularly. Buddha's contribution involves the detachment from filters of thought and language, to immerse oneself in the formless, the precondition to everything we consider real. This is the Gateless Gate eternally present before divisions and distinctions appear.[2] It is the precise function of meditation to facilitate the detachment from self-centered, one-sided thinking, allowing the dust of the world, its forms, concepts, ideas, comparisons, and passions, to settle into a clarity, unmediated by our small minds. There are no categories in the formless.

Gathering information from multiple perspectives expands and deepens any analysis and diminishes the human tendency to be one sided in thinking. The colloquial word for this ability to ride two horses at once—to simultaneously observe reality in multiple modes—is wisdom, and it is wisdom, not simply intelligence or intuition, that is the key agent of conscious human transformation, liberation, and health.

In the final analysis, it is wisdom that awaits the Lone Ranger and Tonto—each in their own way—at the end of the parable and this book.

A PARABLE

When the Lone Ranger had stopped snuffling and dried his eyes, he was exhausted and flopped down before the Buddha like a marionette with cut strings. Regarding him bleakly, the Lone Ranger said, "You got me."

"You got yourself," Buddha observed matter-of-factly, refilling his bowl of tea and pouring one for the Ranger.

"My mom had insane expectations of me," the Lone Ranger whispered. "Nothing I did was good enough. Even my being the most popular hero of all time was kid stuff to her."

"She sounds pitiless," the Buddha remarked. "She must have suffered greatly from that."

There was a pause while the Lone Ranger considered this. "Yeah, I guess she did, too," he said, and they sat in silence awhile. "She made us all suffer," he offered quietly.

"She's been gone a long time," the Buddha offered.

The Lone Ranger sighed deeply. "Oh God," he said, "I've been Rolfed, I did primal screaming. Cary Grant got me to try LSD, okay while it lasted, but . . . I just never knew how to get out of my own way." He moaned and began to cry again.

"Here's something you can do wherever you are," Buddha said. "It's better than LSD because you won't need anything besides yourself. Watch me." He crossed his legs like an Indian at a campfire.

The Lone Ranger tried to imitate him, but his pants were too tight. He leaped up in a rage, ripping off his boots and pants. "Stupid fucking pants," he raged.

The Buddha indicated Tonto's abandoned saddlebags with his thumb. "Jay left a pair of khakis in there. They're probably comfy."

When the Lone Ranger had changed and sat down cross-legged again, the Buddha repeated the instructions he'd offered Tonto. Standing behind the Lone Ranger he placed one of his hands in his lap, palm up, laying the back of the other into it. Touched the tips of his thumbs lightly together in a nice fat circle.

"You can do this in a chair if you have to," Buddha said.

He told the Ranger to adjust his posture—not rigid, just upright, tucking his chin just enough to feel the back of the neck lengthen—and to relax his stomach.

"Count each exhale slowly, up to ten. If you get lost, start over.

After a few minutes you won't need to count. Just maintain an awareness of your breath, thumbs, and posture."

"That's it?" The Lone Ranger inquired. "Really? You're kidding me."

"Nope, that's it," Buddha answered.

"Will you water Silver?" the Ranger asked.

"Will do, buddy," said the Buddha, floating to his feet. "I'll check on you later," and he turned away, walking over toward Silver.

It took the Lone Ranger awhile to get the hang of it, but before long he was absorbed. Scenes from his past rose vividly and evaporated like fog—fights with Clarita and Connie, Sally's tragic death. Recalling unkind things he'd said and done felt like bathing in liquid shame. He remembered the tenderness of the moment he received his daughter from the adoption agency, remembered disappointments, regrets over the careless use of some women, all rising, all passing away, coming from emptiness and returning. His entire life was right there with him, replaying in this present moment and then this one and this . . .

He remembered his heart attack, and the kind nurses at West Hills Hospital and Medical Center—kind not because he was the Lone Ranger but because they lived to help others. His regret at never having pleased his mother by becoming a doctor bloomed in his mind like a black tulip and then evaporated. He remembered his dad warmly, and then his own youthful practice as an acrobat with his buddy Johnny Weissmuller. He smiled at their delight in the strength and prowess of their bodies. He chuckled aloud at some of their early foolishness in LA, before Johnny scored Tarzan and he became the Lone Ranger. His breath quickened to remember the available starlets writhing under the muscular body that had never failed him.

He sat through the afternoon and on through the sunset, not noticing when the Buddha draped a blanket across his shoulders. Neither did he notice his mask slipping gently away from his face and settling softly across his left wrist like the wing of a blackbird. The stars twinkled vividly, reminding him of the rhinestones in the blue velvet dress of that leggy, go-for-broke model he'd samba-ed off the patio and into his bedroom in the Chateau Marmont.

His breathing was slow and regular as a chant, his pulse a drum, the desert around him shadowy and alive with clicks and scratches, the whistles of night birds, the rustling of insects, the yapping of coyotes. The acrid smell of sage was sharp and clean as a razor slice. A rattlesnake crawled across his lap and his pulse never faltered. Strange sounds, spirit sounds—chitters, whoops, flutters—rose and fell in his ears. A wide-eyed desert owl observed him from the tip of a saguaro. Wings whizzed past his forehead. The pain in his legs and back had passed away sometime during the night, and he was grateful because it allowed his concentration to focus more deeply.

At some point, close to dawn, a cricket began to chirp right next to him, extremely loudly and irritatingly insistent. A fury rose within him that this . . . bug! . . . should be disturbing his peace, and an impulse sizzled into his hand to smash it. Before it could fall, however, the cricket's next chirp was so deafening it obliterated every single thought, impulse, or sound in the Lone Ranger's mind, whose interior walls exploded outward and disappeared. The world stopped. Language disappeared and whatever snatched it seized with it every concept, thought, belief, and value judgment he had ever possessed. His "I" disappeared, and all that remained was a pure, centerless awareness. Everything was as it always was but completely free of conception, idea, comparison, or name. The back of his head opened onto infinity; his face had been reduced to two nostrils through which air entered and exited on its own accord, not altogether different from the vastness within and around him.

He had no idea how long he had sat that way before gradually returning to himself. The sun was just rising on the horizon, and honeyed shafts of yellow-red light insinuated themselves under his lids, flooding his retinas and brain with joy at the beauty of the world reassembling before him. He was washed in gratitude to be alive in the midst of such beauty. Squinting, he looked down and saw his mask lying beside him.

He regarded it without emotion, and when a shadow fell across it, he looked up as the Buddha dropped directly into a squat on his haunches, grinning like a fool, and began twirling his forefinger near his ear, as the Lone Ranger had once done about him.

The Lone Ranger grinned back. Offering the mask, he asked, "You want it?"

"Which one?" the Buddha asked.

The Lone Ranger laughed. "The black one."

The Buddha reached out and took it. "Maybe I can use it to cradle my nuts," he said, and they both cracked up.

"What now?" the Lone Ranger asked.

"You tell me," Buddha answered.

"I have no idea. It's all brand new."

"That's a good place to begin. You always liked helping people and traveling around," the Buddha suggested.

"What'll I do about Silver?"

"Why don't you ask him?" Buddha said.

The Lone Ranger looked at Silver, who, at that moment, rose to his feet, shook himself, and walked over, dropping his head to the Lone Ranger's eye level. He seemed to understand that they'd come to a fork in the road. "I'm thinking about going solo," the Lone Ranger said. "How do you feel about that?"

Silver raised his head, looking off toward the distant mesa. The Lone Ranger followed his gaze and noticed a small herd of wild horses about a hundred yards away, marking them watchfully. Standing proudly before them, head erect, was the familiar paint pattern of Tonto's horse, Scout. Silver whinnied, tossing his head, and Scout responded.

The Lone Ranger smiled, and his eyes filled with tears. He took Silver's butter-soft nose into his hands and leaned his forehead against it. They rested together stock-still for a few moments, and then the Lone Ranger said, "What a long strange trip it's been, boy." He sat up straight and for the last time ever shouted, "Hi-yo, Silver!" The stallion rose on his back legs, clawing the sky with his forelegs.

The Lone Ranger grinned at the Buddha. "I just love the shit outta that."

Silver's hooves hit the earth with a thump. He wheeled and pushed off at a full gallop, racing toward Scout. He stopped just once to look back at the Lone Ranger, who saluted him. Silver whinnied and ambled over to Scout, who nuzzled him and led him into the small herd of mares.

"I guess I'm free now," the Lone Ranger said.

"I guess you are," answered the Buddha.

"My name is Jack Carlton Moore," he, previously known as the Lone Ranger, answered, extending his right hand, "but you can call me anything you like."

Buddha gave it a firm shake and laughed. "Hit the road, Jack," he said.

"Should we clean up the camp first?"

"Why not," Buddha said, and they both rose a little creakily, laughing at their ancient bodies.

"Maybe I should be your sidekick, Buddha," Jack said.

"Be your own sidekick, buddy, but we can travel together awhile."

"I'm not actually sure I can eat meat again," Jack replied.

"You'll work it out," replied the Buddha, and the two men began cleaning every trace of their days in the desert together.

"What're we gonna do about the house?" the Lone Ranger asked.

"If you want, take it. It was just little trick to get you guys healthy."

The Lone Ranger considered it a minute. "No," he said, "not really. I always loved traveling around. I would like to show you America, though. I'll bet they've never seen a Buddha.

"You'd be surprised," Buddha replied. "I show up in lots of places. They started off together, heading west.

"We've got to get you some clothes," the Lone Ranger said. "Otherwise, people in California will think you're a freak."

Buddha smiled. "It's obvious you haven't been back in a while, Jack. You're in for some surprises."

As noon's glare abated, they walked off together, leaving the empty house, Tonto's neat little camp and garden, and the Lone Ranger's saddle, mask, and six-guns behind. They walked in silence for most of the afternoon, but toward the end of day, the hour when the shadows lengthen and the mystery hour is about to descend, the Lone Ranger spoke up.

"I've been thinking," the Lone Ranger said. "Have you ever thought about trying show business? We might be able to work something out."

The Buddha did a perfect little soft-shoe shuffle in the sand and laughed with delight.

The Lone Ranger unmasked

Postscript

A young woman named Dolores Taylor from Montana had collected Lone Ranger memorabilia since she was a child. Her passion continued through University of Colorado medical school. She remained haunted by the Lone Ranger's ethical commitment even after med school at Stanford and later as a Harvard Fellow.

One day she was wandering about in the desert (departing from the Montana forests where she usually hiked) and came upon the saddle, pistols, and mask the Lone Ranger had left behind. She recognized them instantly. Her eyes filled with tears, and she dropped to her knees in gratitude to God, feeling that her discovery was a heavenly reward for her lifelong diligence and study of the Lone Ranger and his inherent goodness. When she died, she left her entire collection to the Lone Ranger Museum in Waco, Texas. If you don't believe me, google it. You can see it all there, today, which should prove that everything about this story is true.

Acknowledgments

Both of my previous books were first read and critiqued by "the two Terrys"—author Terry Bisson and filmmaker Terry Strauss. This one was no exception. Bisson's eye for form, clarity, and superfluous verbiage is acute, and he has never failed to demonstrate the possibility of a thinner manuscript than the one I delivered to him nor failed to catch any deviations from my stated intentions for the book. Strauss asks the deep questions about content and intuits every point where I left no marker and the reader might be led astray or misunderstand.

The magician who appeared in the last moments of the third act as I was about to self-publish this book is now my agent, Joe Kulin, a gift from another friend, Brenton MacKinnon, who made the match. It was Kulin who unerringly connected me with the wonderful folks at Inner Traditions, and my gratitude to all of the above is unbounded.

I'd also like to acknowledge a debt to Sherman Alexie and his book, *The Lone Ranger and Tonto Fistfight in Heaven*. We probably perceived different Lone Ranger and Tonto, but he was the first to rescue the two of them from the archtype dustheap. I'd also urge readers to look at his film *Smoke Signals*. I'd like to express my deep gratitude in particular to my dharma brother Tony Head, whose meticulous reading of the text and thoughtful notes were invaluable. And lastly to my longtime dharma brother David Chadwick whose labors to keep Suzuki-roshi's lectures in print and available on Cuke.com have been a wellspring of nourishment to me. Many thanks for his close reading of the text and his catching numerous errors of fact. A deep bow of gratitude.

PETER COYOTE,
SEBASTOPOL, CALIFORNIA

Notes

AUTHOR'S PREFACE.
A TRUE HOLIDAY FROM SELF-CONSCIOUSNESS

1. For a basic primer on Buddhism, see Thich Nhat Hanh, "Dharma Talk: The Eightfold Path," *Mindfulness Bell* 13 (Spring 1995), www.mindfulnessbell .org/archive/2016/02/dharma-talk-the-eightfold-path-2; and Walpola Sri Rahula, "The Noble Eightfold Path," *Tricycle: The Buddhist Review,* 2019, https://tricycle.org/magazine/noble-eightfold-path.

CHAPTER 1.
LOSING MYSELF

1. Norman Fischer, "Nothing Holy," *Shambala Sun,* March 2004.
2. I chronicle this period in my first book: Peter Coyote, *Sleeping Where I Fall: A Chronicle,* 3rd ed. (Berkeley, Calif.: Counterpoint Press, 2015; first published 1998).
3. There's an extensive discussion of this house in Coyote, *Sleeping Where I Fall.*

CHAPTER 2.
THE WHEEL'S SPINNING, BUT
THE GERBIL'S GONE

1. David Halberstam, *The Making of a Quagmire: America and Vietnam during the Kennedy Era,* rev ed. (Lanham, Md.: Rowman and Littlefield), 128.

2. "The Burning Monk," 1963, Rare Historical Photos (website), June 23, 2015.

CHAPTER 5.
TRICKING AND TRAPPING THE SELF

1. Keith Johnston, *Impro: Improvisation and the Theatre* (London: Routledge, 2015; first published 1979), 144.

CHAPTER 6.
INVITING THE SHOCK OF RECOGNITION

1. Richard Schechner, *Between Theater and Anthropology* (Philadelphia: University of Pennsylvania Press, 1985).

CHAPTER 10.
MASKED IN A HALL OF MIRRORS

1. Carlos Castaneda, *Journey to Ixtlan: The Lessons of Don Juan* (New York: Simon and Schuster, New York, 1972), 32–33, 34.

CHAPTER 12.
THE MASKS OF LANGUAGE

1. Bruce Fingerhut, "I Gotta Use Words When I Talk to You," Rectifying Names (blog), April 23, 2012, St. Augustine's Press, www.staugustine.net/blogs /rectify-names-a-blog-on-publishing/i-gotta-use-words-when-i-talk-to-you.

CHAPTER 14.
BUDDHA'S EMPTY HANDS

1. For a lovely explanation see Steven Goodman, "On Adhidarma," from Goodman, *The Buddhist Psychology of Awakening*, Shambhala Publications, YouTube video, 2:45, April 21, 2018, www.youtube.com/watch?v =cRfTKzfcPPc.
2. Shunryu Suzuki, *Zen Mind, Beginner's Mind: Informal Talks on Zen Meditation and Practice* (Berkeley, Calif.: Shambhala, 2011), 109.

CHAPTER 15.
THE DEVIL YOU DON'T KNOW

1. This experience and its immediate aftermath are described in my second book: Peter Coyote, *The Rainman's Third Cure: An Irregular Education* (Berkeley, Calif.: Counterpoint Press, 2015).
2. Hakuin Zenji, *Complete Poison Blossoms from a Thicket of Thorn: The Zen Records of Hakuin Zenji,* trans. Norman Waddell (Berkeley, Calif.: Counterpoint Press, 2017), 685.

CHAPTER 16.
EVEN BUDDHA CAN BETRAY YOU

1. Carlos Castaneda, *A Separate Reality* (New York: Simon and Schuster, 1971), 107.

CHAPTER 17.
LOCATING AND LISTENING TO YOUR TRUE SELF

1. Dalai Lama, *Beyond Religion: Ethics for a Whole World* (New York: Houghton Mifflin Harcourt, 2011).
2. See Koun Yamada, *The Gateless Gate: The Classic Book of Zen Koans* (Boston: Wisdom, 2004).

Suggested Reading

Basically, Zen Buddhism is a *practice* that does not require over much intellection, but understanding the minds of masters of meditation and their reflections on Buddhist practice and thought can provide inspiration, cautions, and invaluable guidance. I suggest the following books for those who'd like to explore the subject more deeply.

Aitken, Robert. *Taking the Path of Zen*. New York: North Point Press, 1982. Aitken is a teacher of mine from the Rinzai (koan) tradition. A clear and simple how-to book, which I've suggested to many people who have found it useful.

Anderson, Robert. *Being Upright: Zen Meditation and the Bodhisattva Precepts*. Berkeley, Calif.: Rodmell Press, 2000. Reb Anderson, a senior priest and teacher at Green Gulch Monastery, is one of my first dharma friends and an exemplar of Buddhist practice.

Dalai Lama. *Awakening the Mind, Lightening the Heart*. San Francsico: HarperSanFranciso, 1995. His Holiness the Dalai Lama is a global spiritual influence of unblemished reputation and rectitude. Hard to say enough about him.

———. *Beyond Religion: Ethics for a Whole World*. New York: Houghton Mifflin Harcourt, 2011.

Okumura, Shohaku. *Living by Vow: A Practical Introduction to Eight Essential Zen Chants and Texts*. Somerville, Mass.: Wisdom, 2012.

Don't be put off by the title. Okumura is a teacher of great subtlety and wisdom, very familiar with American students.

Suzuki, Shunryu. *Not Always So: Practicing the True Spirit of Zen*. New York: HarperOne, 2009. Suzuki-roshi, founder of my lineage in America, continues to be a profound influence to this day, decades after his passing, and his lessons blossom across the country in numerous Zen centers and study groups.

———. *Zen Mind, Beginner's Mind: Informal Talks on Zen Meditation and Practice*. Berkeley, Calif.: Shambhala, 2011. This is an extremely accessible book; more than a million copies have been sold. It is also available in an audio book that I narrated.

Thich Nhat Hanh. *The Heart of the Buddha's Teaching: Transforming Suffering into Peace, Joy, and Liberation*. New York: Harmony, 2015. A widely revered Vietnamese teacher of profound gentleness, Thich Nhat Hanh was once the recipient of death threats from nearly every faction during America's war in Vietnam.

Finally, some books on practice that demonstrate the practical application and utility of meditating Buddhism, which I find myself recommending often. Two of them are by my teacher Lewis Richmond.

Chödrön, Pema. *When Things Fall Apart: Heart Advice for Difficult Times*. Berkeley, Calif.: Shambhala, 2005. Chödrön is a woman teacher in the lineage of the late Chögyam Trungpa, a renowned Tibetan teacher and author.

Cohen, Darlene. *The One Who Is Not Busy: Connecting with Work in a Deeply Satisfying Way*. Layton, Utah: Gibbs Smith, 2004. Cohen is a wonderful teacher and friend from my lineage.

Richmond, Lewis. *Aging as a Spiritual Practice: A Contemplative Guide to Growing Older and Wiser*. New York: Gotham Books, 2012

———. *Work as a Spiritual Practice: A Practical Buddhist Approach to Inner Growth and Satisfaction on the Job*. New York: Harmony, 2000.

Think of these books as conversations with wise and loving uncles and aunts. They are neither the Bible, Koran, nor Torah, neither are they commandments from omniscient beings. They offer hard-won advice from men and women who have pursued self-knowledge and self-control to extraordinary degrees. Take what you can from them, and if you encounter something that gives you difficulty, well, meditate on it. A deep bow.

People interested in learning more about mask workshops are invited to contact me at

beth@wdprod.com

for details and scheduling, and they can go to my YouTube channel to see a half-hour video of one of the classes mentioned in the book.

Youtube.com/c/HoshoPeterCoyoteDharma.

Index